Wood Pellet Grill
and **Smoker Cookbook**
for **Beginners**

ANDREW
KOSTER

Wood Pellet Grill and Smoker Cookbook

FOR BEGINNERS

EASY RECIPES FOR BACKYARD BARBECUE EXCELLENCE

PHOTOGRAPHY BY DARREN MUIR

ROCKRIDGE
PRESS

To those affected by the
West Coast fires of summer 2020.

For general information on our other products and services or to obtain technical support, please contact our Customer Care Department within the United States at (866) 744-2665, or outside the United States at (510) 253-0500.

Rockridge Press publishes its books in a variety of electronic and print formats. Some content that appears in print may not be available in electronic books, and vice versa.

TRADEMARKS: Rockridge Press and the Rockridge Press logo are trademarks or registered trademarks of Callisto Media Inc. and/or its affiliates, in the United States and other countries, and may not be used without written permission. All other trademarks are the property of their respective owners. Rockridge Press is not associated with any product or vendor mentioned in this book.

Interior and Cover Designer: Brieanna Felschow
Art Producer: Samantha Ulban
Editor: Claire Yee
Production Editor: Jenna Dutton
Production Manager: Riley Hoffman

Photography © 2021 Darren Muir. Food styling by Yolanda Muir. Author photo credit courtesy of Chanelle Koster.

Paperback ISBN: 978-1-64876-682-4
eBook ISBN: 978-1-64876-179-9
R0

CONTENTS

INTRODUCTION

My origin story with pellet grills begins right around the time I was born. My father, George Koster, was an employee of Traeger Industries back when Joe Traeger developed the first pellet grill in the mid-1980s. Since the inception of pellet grills, my backyards have been filled with their smoke.

My experience with pellet barbecue didn't end there—not by a long shot. Growing up, I worked odd jobs, from building hardware kits to shoveling lava rock for the early drain pans, at the old Traeger barn in Mt. Angel, Oregon. After graduating from Oregon State University, I stepped fully into a career in barbecue. I was the customer service manager at Traeger Grills from 2011 to 2016, and from 2017 to 2018, I held the same position at Dansons, maker of Pit Boss grills. Since then, I've moved over to the product development side of things, and I'm currently the quality manager at Dansons. I have another book on pellet grilling, *Master the Wood Pellet Grill: A Cookbook to Smoke Meats and More Like a Pro*, which is a great companion to this book.

Beyond my professional experience, I honestly just love to grill! I cook everything on my pellet grills, and I'm always trying new things. I grill almost every day, and I often document it on my Instagram @andrewkoster. I don't stop at the basics—I try plenty of things that you might not expect to see on a pellet grill. Baking is one of my favorite things to do on a pellet grill, and we will dive headfirst into it later in this book.

To me, the magic of the pellet grill is that anyone can pick up the skill set with a minimal amount of practice. In my years of working in customer service, I talked to countless first-time pellet grillers, and I've witnessed many of them become experts.

The recipes and tips in this book are a result not only of my own years spent pellet grilling, but also of time helping others learn to master their own grill. If this book does its job, it will help you better understand your pellet grill, and I hope you come out of it with a new expertise and experiences that shape your path to becoming a pitmaster.

PART
One

LIGHTING THE FIRE

CHAPTER ONE

GETTING TO KNOW YOUR WOOD PELLET GRILL AND SMOKER

THE FIRST step toward mastering the pellet grill is an obvious one: learning how your grill works. Once you have a basic understanding of how your grill functions, you'll have no problem making the recipes in this book and others as well. In this chapter, we'll dive into the various parts of the grill, how it works, what it can do, and what you can do to get the most out it. As the most versatile grill on the market, the pellet grill will allow you to show off your skills not only as a griller but also as a smoker, chef, and even baker.

The Easiest Route to Barbecue Perfection

Good barbecuers are among the most demanding and knowledgeable characters in the world of cooking. Their attention to each and every detail of a cook—from the cut of meat to the temperature to the cooking apparatuses used throughout—makes them some of the most obsessive cooks you will ever meet. They'll customize their pits, be engrossed over meat grades, and have cupboards overflowing with spices, all part of their quest for the perfect cook.

Styles of barbecue can vary greatly worldwide, but traditional low and slow barbecue is most commonly the method of choice among the world's best, most seasoned grillers. The term "low and slow" refers to cooking over a low temperature for a long period of time. This method allows pitmasters to achieve a consistent smoke that will deeply penetrate the meat and drastically affect the flavor.

Pellet grills are relative newcomers to the barbecue scene—the first model was invented by Joe Traeger in the small town of Mt. Angel, Oregon, in the mid-1980s. Since then, they've quickly become a top choice among seasoned grillers and newcomers alike. This is no doubt due to their ease of use and efficiency, allowing for great flavors without the hours of babysitting a grill. Many grillers have found that with a pellet grill, you can do the same grilling, roasting, and barbecuing you'd do on a traditional grill, plus more.

Pellet grills have become the fastest-growing appliance in the industry, and for good reason. It's not only entry-level grillers; even the most experienced pitmasters are starting to opt for it as well. You'll find pellet grills in the backyards of competition cooks, social media stars, cookbook authors, and more. There are even pellet-grill categories at many of the annual barbecue competitions around the world.

Although there will always be a place for traditional barbecue grills, pellet grills have made quite a name for themselves, and there's no question why. They use the same hardwoods found in old-school barbecuing to create similar—and often better—flavor with far more ease. It's no wonder that we've seen the explosion in popularity of the pellet grill in recent years, and the industry will only continue to grow for years to come.

The Wide World of Pellet Grills and Smokers

For years, pellet grilling was associated with one name: Traeger. Joe Traeger developed the first pellet grill, and Traeger Industries held a patent on the design into the 2000s. Once the patent lifted, many smaller brands popped up, but for a while afterward, the vast majority of pellet grills on back porches were still Traegers.

In recent years, all that has changed. Nowadays, there are many more big-name players in the pellet-grilling game, and each one brings something different to the table. Brands like Pit Boss, Green Mountain, and Louisiana Grills have led the way, and even established brands in the grill industry, like Weber and Broil King, have added pellet grills to their existing charcoal and gas lineups. These emerging brands have brought an array of modern features to a decades-old system.

Innovations from brands like Weber and Green Mountain have led to the emergence of pellet grills with Bluetooth and WiFi connectivity. Meanwhile, Pit Boss and Louisiana Grills have introduced pellet grills with open-flame capabilities. Hopper dumps, ash cleanouts, shelves, and service-ability improvements all have come about in recent years, making the life of the pellet griller better than it has ever been. There are even multifuel combination units on the market today, giving the griller secondary cooking surfaces like gas grills and griddles. Additionally, improvements to the mechanical components have given grills a longer lifespan and have created a more consistent, reliable grilling experience.

Though we've seen substantial changes in pellet grills and their technology over the years, pellet grills at their core rely on the same original system: an auger-fed system that pushes wood pellets to a fan-aided fire pot (or burn grate). Most pellet grills and smokers also have an igniter, which lights the grill's fire during the initial start-up, but after that, the fire is self-sustaining. If you understand the grill in terms of these basic elements (and don't worry, we'll go over them in more detail in the next section), you'll have no problem creating incredible dishes using your pellet grill.

The Parts of the Smoker

To even the most seasoned of grillers, the pellet grill at first glance might look like any other grill. Pellet grills are typically made in the same familiar shapes and styles as those of of traditional grills and pits, but it is what's under the hood that makes them different. The pellet grill is a fully automated system, feeding and maintaining a consistent fire for great-tasting, professional-level results.

As I mentioned in the previous section, on a basic level, most pellet grills are actually quite similar. The standard pellet grill consists of a few main components: the control board and temperature probe, auger and drive motor, fan, and igniter. These parts work together to light and maintain a fire, all while keeping the temperatures at a consistent and controllable level.

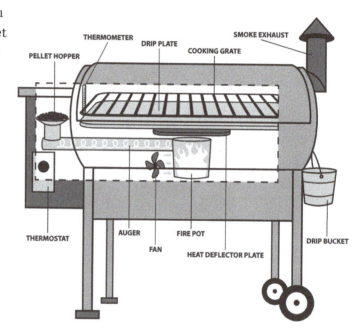

Hopper

A pellet grill requires hardwood pellets as a source of fuel. These pellets come in bags or boxes ranging in size from 10 to 40 pounds. Because different cooks can require as little as a few cups of pellets and as many as a full 20-pound bag, pellet grills have a hopper to hold these pellets. The hopper has angled walls that funnel the pellets directly into the auger by means of gravity.

Auger

Most every pellet grill uses an auger-fed system, originally used in the wood pellet stoves that started to heat homes around the world starting in the 1970s. The corkscrew-shaped auger is connected to a motor that turns the auger to deliver pellets from the hopper to the fire pot and, finally, to the fire.

Fire Pot/Burn Grate

The fire pot (or burn grate) is where the action happens. Pellets are delivered by way of the auger to the fire pot or burn grate, where they are ignited. Fire pots are cylindrical vessels, while burn grates typically have a V shape. Most pellet grills manufactured in the early 2000s or later include a steel or ceramic igniter to light the pellets to start the fire.

These days, many fire pots and burn grates are removable. It's extremely important for proper functionality that this piece is installed to the manufacturer's specifications.

Fan

To have a fire you need two things: fuel and air. To create the clean, intense fire of a pellet grill, a fan delivers air directly to the burning pellets. Some models even have multiple fans for this purpose.

Heat Deflector

Heat deflectors are used in Traeger, Green Mountain, Country Smokers, and other pellet grills. The heat deflector sits directly over the fire pot, diffusing the heat and flame to prevent hot spots and provide better convection, creating a more evenly heated surface.

Not all pellet grills use a heat deflector. Pellet grills that have any type of open-flame system, like those made by Weber and Pit Boss, do not use a heat deflector. On some grills, especially smaller portable grills, the heat deflector is a part of the drain pan.

Drain Pan

Because most pellet grilling is done over an indirect flame, it can be a greasy event. Most pellet grills include a drain pan to guide grease off the grill, and more importantly keep it away from the fire. Drain pans are typically slanted pieces of steel that catch the grease so it can drain out into a bucket.

Some pellet grills, like those from Pit Boss and Louisiana Grills, let users open the drain pan to cook with direct flame. Weber even has its own "Flavorizer" bar system that allows you to use an open flame throughout the grill.

RTD/Thermocouple

Pellet grills use a resistance temperature detector (RTD) or thermocouple to detect the temperature inside the chamber and pass that information to the controller. This temperature detection device is what makes temperature control possible. Without an RTD or thermocouple, your controller would have no idea what's going on inside the grill.

Controller

The controller is a circuit board usually located on the hopper—think of it as the brains of the grill. The controller does what it implies: It controls the amount of fuel and air being delivered to your grill's fire pot. It adjusts the pellet feed rate by turning the auger motor on and off, and it determines the fan speed. While most grills use a single-speed fan, newer grills sometimes come with a multispeed fan to aid in smoke creation.

One Grill, Endless Possibilities

The pellet grill is unmatched in the grilling industry in terms of versatility. The indirect flame and the air-induced, auger-fed fire untether the griller from many of the restraints of traditional grilling. From smoking to baking to braising to searing, almost any cooking style is possible on your pellet grill.

Smoking

There's no denying that pellet grills are great at smoking. The smoke from a pellet grill is light and crisp. It packs flavor, but not that heavy creosote taste you get from other forms of smoking. To many, the smoking capability is a huge selling point of the pellet grill—in fact, people often somewhat misleadingly use the terms "pellet grill" and "smoker" interchangeably. To create smoke, the controller restricts the auger feed, leading to small temperature swings that create smoke.

That's a key thing to be aware of when using your pellet grill as a smoker: When your grill smokes, you'll see small swings in temperature. Many new pellet grillers mistakenly panic when this happens, thinking their grills are malfunctioning. When you see this, don't be alarmed—these swings are normal.

You can smoke everything from fish to brisket on a pellet grill. The smoky meats that we usually associate with barbecue here in the United States, such as brisket, ribs, and pulled pork, can all be smoked on your pellet grill, just as you'd get them at your favorite barbecue joint.

Grilling

Grilling is what comes to mind when you think of cooking old-school hot dogs and hamburgers. It refers to cooking over high heat for a short period of time. You can grill on a pellet grill with ease, as pellet grills can reach temperatures of 400°F to 600°F. At such high temperatures, a restaurant-quality home-cooked steak can be ready in minutes.

Thanks to the drain pain, you can grill pork chops and chicken thighs over high heat on your pellet grill without worrying about causing a grease fire. Nowadays, some pellet grills are made with either an opening drain pan or no drain pan at all, making it possible to sear and char-grill over a direct flame, a feature I've seen requested in pellet grills for years.

Baking

If you haven't tried baking on a pellet grill, you are in for a treat. Because of the convection created from the pellet grill's induction fan, you can bake on your pellet grill as easily as with an indoor oven. Anything from wood-fired bread to marionberry pie can be done on your pellet grill.

Baking on your grill will also give you a flavor that an electric oven simply cannot. It's not overbearing, but you'll find you can detect a hint of smoky flavor in whatever baked goods you make on the grill. Wood-fired pizza, cookies, cinnamon rolls, and so much more are all at your fingertips with your pellet grill.

Braising

Braising refers to the process of cooking dry over high heat before finishing using liquid. Braising probably isn't the first technique that comes to mind when we think of grilling, but it's actually used often. Your pellet grill makes braising an easy and enjoyable task. Short ribs, jambalaya, shrimp, and many more recipes are all opportunities to braise using your pellet grill.

Roasting

Roasting is another traditional form of barbecue that can be done easily using a pellet grill. Roasting refers to cooking over high heat, often for a longer period of time. Roasting on a pellet grill will give you all the same benefits of cooking at high heat on other grills—that perfect crust and color, great flavor, and juiciness—without the worry over burning your meat or drying it out.

As with baking, with roasting, the magic is in the convection. Thanks to the convection element, we can heat all areas of the meat evenly. This method allows us to cook up beautiful roasted chickens without a rotisserie and juicy pork tenderloins without any turning or flipping.

Grill Buddies

One of my favorite things about pellet grilling is that it allows me to cook multiple items in one place with minimal bells and whistles. Don't get me wrong, there are tons of awesome accessories out there, and I'm often tempted to try out even the silliest accessories (my wife hates that).

That said, you really only need a few tools for world-class grilling. Listed below are some of my favorite tools to help get the job done.

Equipment Essentials

Instant-read thermometer: If you buy just one these tools, make it a thermometer. With meat, you should always cook to temperature—don't just rely on the estimated time in a recipe. Using an instant-read thermometer will make you an immensely better cook.

Tongs: You'll use tongs for nearly everything on the grill. You don't need huge tongs, though; I use a simple pair I picked up for a dollar at the local general store.

Gloves: A good pair of heat-resistant barbecue or leather gloves are a must-have for any griller. Most of us have the scars to show you why.

Large metal spatula: An oversized flat metal spatula will take the hassle out of moving large cuts. Your spatula should have a giant head and be heavy duty, made to move your biggest cuts.

Basting brush: Basting brushes are used a ton during grilling, whether you're basting a chicken or brushing sauce on ribs.

Cast-iron skillet: Of all the cookware you might want for your grill, the cast-iron skillet is a must-have. From searing to braising, I promise you'll make good use of it. My favorite cast-iron piece is a 12-inch skillet with two handles made by Petromax.

Barbecue knives: Having a good, sharp set of knives will save you time and energy. I regularly use slicing and carving knives, boning knives, and a good knife for slicing brisket. (I have the Victorinox Fibrox Pro chef's knife.)

Cutting board: I have a beautiful live-edge cutting board made of a solid piece of wood, but any quality cutting board will do.

Knife sharpener: Unsharpened knives are a mess that makes more messes. Make sure your knives are sharp—sharp knives are safer than dull ones, and you'll impress your friends when you cut through your next brisket like butter.

Drain pan or bucket liners: These liners go inside your pellet grill's existing drain pan or bucket. Just switch out the liner every few grills.

Nice-to-Haves

Injector: An injector is basically a syringe you use to inject flavor into your meat. I mainly use my injector for pork butts and poultry. You can usually find a standard injector or syringe at your local grocery store, but a quality one from a barbecue manufacturer will make the job cleaner and easier.

Cast-iron Dutch oven and roaster: This is another invaluable piece of cast iron that can be used on your grill. Stews, roasts, breads, and more can all be made on a pellet grill with a good Dutch oven with a lid.

Nitrile gloves: I use these at nearly every step along the way, from prep to cleanup. As a loyal fan of Oregon State athletics, I've been known to alternate between black and orange. Go Beavers!

Combo grilling tool: Here I'm referring to a spatula-tongs combo tool. It's a total game changer, allowing you to keep your grip on meat while lifting it. I use this tool for everything from steaks to whole chickens.

Cut-resistant gloves: No one wants to ruin a good barbecue session by cutting off the tip of their finger. This advice comes to you from a man missing the tip of his left index finger.

Meat claws: Quality meat claws work wonders for shredding chicken, duck, and other meats. An important note: These should never be used for pulled pork! If your pork is too hot to pull apart with your hands, then it needs to keep resting.

COOKER CLEANING AND CARE

Though pellet grills are overall easier to use than traditional grills, they still require the cleaning and occasional maintenance that you would expect with any barbecue appliance. Since they use an indirect flame, pellet grills can get greasy. I clean out my drain pan after every few cooks, or after every really greasy cook (like a whole chicken or hamburgers).

I recommend investing in drain pan and bucket liners to save time on cleanup. The liners are so much easier to slip in than the potential messes you might be dealing with otherwise. If your grill doesn't come with a drain pan, use a disposable aluminum pan to catch grease from longer smokes, such as pulled pork or brisket.

Every 60 to 80 pounds of pellets or so, I recommend a quick but full clean of your grill. This does not need to be a heavy cleaning—just enough to remove the ash and keep the grease in check. Vacuum out the fire pot and the bottom of the grill. Change out your drain pan liner or scrape it off. Wipe the grill down using a light degreaser or citrus-based cleaner.

Always protect your grill and accessories from the weather, particularly from moisture. Wood pellets are compressed wood fibers, so they have extremely low moisture content. If pellets come into contact with moisture of any kind, they can and likely will expand and disintegrate. This can not only create a poor cooking experience—moisture-affected pellets will burn at significantly cooler temperatures—but it can also create ignition problems and jams in your grill's auger

Use a cover issued by your grill's manufacturer to protect your grill from the elements. When not in use, store the grill in a dry area, like a garage or shed. If you're going a significant amount of time without using your grill—a few weeks or longer—remove all the pellets from the hopper and run the grill out to empty it.

Troubleshooting

Pellet grilling is pretty easy to get a handle on, but as you get acclimated, you might run into a few of these common bumps in the road. Here are my recommendations in the event that you find yourself having trouble with your grill.

Temperature swings: Most often, the key to dealing with temperature swings is patience. Why? Because we make a pellet grill smoke by swinging its temperature.

Even experienced grillers can have trouble getting used to temperature swings when making the switch to pellet grilling. Though swings are dreaded in traditional smokers, they're actually a necessary part of the pellet-grilling process. Frequent swings of around 25°F in either direction are normal when pellet grilling at low temperatures. Unless you're baking, they'll have no negative effect on your cooking.

The way that most pellet grills control temperature and smoke are by turning the auger feed off and on, dropping new pellets on the hot coals. When the auger is dumping pellets and begins smoking, the temperature drops. Once that smoke disappears, you hear the fire roar back up, and the temperature rises. This is the reason that pellet grill temperatures swing, but it's also the reason we get that amazing smoke.

Grease fires: Grease fires are most often caused by dirty drain pans, but other factors can also lead to flare-ups. To avoid grease fires, it's easiest to first clean your drain pan and grill grates, and wipe down the inside of the grill with a light degreaser. If this doesn't solve the fire issues, follow the fire to find where the grease may be pooling (or otherwise not draining) inside the grill. Grease buildup and broken sealants are both likely causes for grease fires.

Soot on food: If you're noticing soot, there is probably something interrupting your airflow. Check that your fan, typically under the hopper, is free of blockages, and make sure that the air intake area is clear. The fan of a pellet grill should almost always be turning, so if the fan on your grill has stopped, there's probably an issue.

Low temperatures: Low temperatures are almost always the result of poor-quality fuel. Wood pellets that have been sitting on a shelf or in a hopper for too long can start to go bad, and you might not notice until you're cooking. Good pellets should be glossy; dusty-looking pellets tend to be moisture-tainted, which will make it difficult for them to reach high temperatures.

If the wood pellets are not the issue, you might just need some simple maintenance on your grill. If your grill's fire pot has holes that weren't originally there or have gotten bigger, the fire pot probably needs to be replaced. Check the airflow, and make sure there are no obstructions. Clean your grill's fan—clean blades produce more air.

Grill going out: If your grill loses its fire during a cook, don't restart it! Remove everything from the inside of the grill and make there are no unburned pellets in the fire pot. If there are unburned pellets, remove them before you restart the grill.

A grill going out is typically caused by low pellets on a long cook. The pellets may sit on the sides of the hopper and not feed into the auger correctly, which will cause the grill to go out. If you address these issues and your grill continues to go out, even on a semifrequent basis, there's likely something else at play. At that point, I would suggest reaching out to the manufacturer.

PELLET-GRILLED CORN ON THE COB ★ 116

CHAPTER TWO

COOKING WITH YOUR WOOD PELLET GRILL AND SMOKER

IN THIS chapter, we're going to go over the nitty-gritty of how to use your pellet grill. We'll dive into the basics and start to mosey our way into a few pro tips. Truly digging in and understanding the grill is going to help you immensely in your growth as a griller.

Wood Is Good

Hardwood pellets are the small, pencil eraser–shaped pieces that are used to fuel your wood pellet grill. Pellets are manufactured by taking hardwood sawdust or fibers and compacting them with enough force and pressure that they hold together. Barbecue pellets are 100 percent hardwood, with no glues or additives. Some brands use oil as a way to add flavor to their pellets, while others create blends and even use charcoal for flavoring.

Cooking with wood pellets makes for cleaner, easier, and more flavorful results compared to charcoal or gas grilling. In the early days of pellet grilling, those of us in the industry would tell customers that they were getting the best of both worlds: the taste of charcoal with the ease of gas. Neither of these assertions is completely true, but the general idea translates, offering a window into why pellet grills continue to grow in popularity to this day.

Once turned on, your grill will drop pellets into the fire pot, where a superheated igniter is waiting. Your grill will produce a thick, heavy smoke that will dissipate once the fire has been lit in the pot. When cooking at different settings, your grill's controller will adjust the frequency at which pellets are introduced to the fire. This frequency will affect the strength of the fire and the amount of smoke. At lower settings, 180°F through 275°F, the grill will tend to have longer, wider swings of smoke and temperature. At higher temperatures, the amount of smoke reduces, as do the swings. This is because at higher temperatures we are feeding pellets into the fire more frequently, thereby keeping a steady, roaring fire. Remember that there's always a fire in a pellet grill, even on the lowest smoke setting—it's just a matter of how big that fire is.

Just as the pitmasters who use charcoal or hardwood logs, you can control your pellet grill's flame, heat, and smoke by adjusting the rate and amount of fuel that is introduced to the fire. And just like with other fuels, you can change the type of pellet wood you use to change up the flavor. Mesquite and hickory are known for their bold flavor, while fruitwoods have a subtle sweetness. Refer to the "Picking the Perfect Pellet" chart to choose the type of pellet flavor you prefer.

PICKING THE PERFECT PELLET

WOOD	FLAVOR	USE IT TO COOK
Hickory	Heavy smoke, woodsy	All meats, nuts, fish, cheese, vegetables
Mesquite	Heavy smoke, creosote	Beef, poultry, fish, cheese, game
Alder	Subtle smoke, sweet	Beef, poultry, fish, baking, vegetables, game
Maple	Mild smoke	Pork, poultry, fish, baking, vegetables, game
Oak	Smoky	Beef, fish, game
Apple	Light smoke, sweet	Beef, pork, poultry, baking, vegetables
Pecan	Light smoke, nutty	Beef, pork, poultry, baking, vegetables
Charcoal	Smoky, charcoal	Beef, poultry, vegetables, game
Competition blends	Smoky, sweet	Everything

How to Use Your Wood Pellet Grill and Smoker

Once you master the basics, the pellet grill is extremely simple—most often, the grill will do the heavy lifting for you. Your general cooking process will rely on the same fundamental techniques. Here are some basic cooking steps (and tips) for the typical cook on your pellet grill.

STEP 1

GRILL START-UP Start-up is probably the most important phase of a pellet-grill cook, but it's also the most frequently misunderstood. This goes back to something I mentioned earlier: *There is always a fire in a running grill.* To get that fire started, we run the grill hard, and it can get hot. During this start-up period, which can range anywhere from 5 to 15 minutes, it's not uncommon for a grill to swing upwards of 300°F, something that alarms many people who are new to the pellet-grilling game.

Most pellet grills are started at the lowest setting with the lid open, though this is not always the case. The grill will produce heavy white smoke that will dissipate in a short time, signaling a fire has been successfully lit. Once the fire is lit, you can shut the lid, adjust the dial to your selected temperature, and get started cooking.

STEP 2

FOOD PREPARATION In order to start our pellet grill, we have to run the auger for a long enough time to ensure a fire is lit in the fire pot. This process can cause high temperature swings just after start-up. This has actually created a habit in me and many other early pellet-grill adopters: While we waited for the temperature of the grill to drop to an acceptable smoke range after start-up, we do our food prep. If you're finding your grill has a temperature upswing upon start-up, you can do the same.

Make sure you have your tools, dishes, and whatever you want to cook ready to go so you can work efficiently while the pellet grill is doing its work. There are some recipes in which food preparation is best done further ahead of time, so take a quick glance at a recipe to see if you need to plan for prep time. If you're doing a quick cook, though, the grill start-up time provides you a great window to do quick preps like for strip steaks and chicken breasts.

STEP 3

PLACING FOOD ON THE GRILL First, always wait for your grill to preheat to your desired temperature before you put anything on the grill. You don't want to burn something during a start-up temperature swing. Second, you should be aware of any hot spots on the grill. You can test your grill's hot spots by cooking a batch of potatoes and seeing how they cook at different places on the grill. Overall, hotspots are easy to find and work with. While steaks and pork chops thrive in hot spots, you should avoid them when baking. If your grill doesn't have an open-flame option, you can take advantage of the hot spots and the edge of the grill to get more direct heat for char-grilling.

Right when you put your food on the grill is when you should set up any meat probes or timers. Many newer pellet grills have these features included in the controller, but if your grill doesn't, there are plenty of after market remote timers and thermometers available.

STEP 4

TURNING/FLIPPING/BASTING During your cooks, you'll often work directly with the meat, veggies, or other preps. Time can sneak up on you, so always keep your tools nearby, including good grilling spatulas, multi-tools with tongs, and a basting brush. Many grills come with shelves and hooks for this very reason.

STEP 5

CHECKING MEAT TEMPERATURE *This is important*, and I'll repeat it throughout the book: Always cooking your meat to temperature is the most vital thing you can do on your way to becoming a true grill master. This is necessary to make sure your meat reaches the necessary temperature to prevent foodborne illness—plus, overcooking your meat can dry it out and make for an underwhelming cut. Always have a meat thermometer ready, and when following recipes, always pay attention to the temperature requirement rather than just the estimated time.

STEP 6

PULLING FOOD FROM THE GRILL AND SHUTDOWN Make sure to be careful when pulling items off the grill, especially when working with more tender cooks, such as fish. Always shut your grill down immediately, before you forget. It's also easiest to clean your grill grates while they're still warm. Use balled-up aluminum foil or a wood scraper to clean off the gunk. Unless your grill's owner's manual says otherwise, I always recommend keeping the lid shut to prevent additional airflow.

Backyard Barbecue All-Stars

Your pellet grill is ready for all your favorite barbecue classics and so much more. The way your pellet grill functions makes long cooks like brisket and pulled pork a breeze—the automatic feed allows you to kick back and relax while the meat is cooking away. At the same time, your grill also gets hot enough to give you some of the best-ever wood-fired vegetables, from potatoes to corn to blistered Brussels sprouts. If that wasn't enough, you can also bake using your pellet grill and get even better results than you might in the kitchen. Breads, cakes, and the like can be cooked outside on hot summer days.

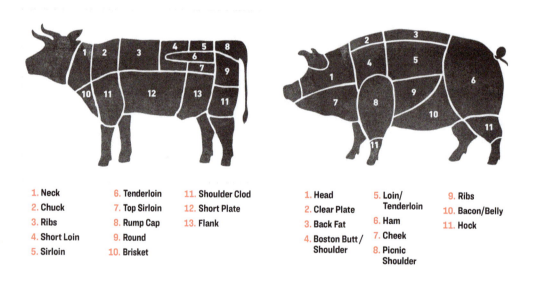

1. Neck	6. Tenderloin	11. Shoulder Clod
2. Chuck	7. Top Sirloin	12. Short Plate
3. Ribs	8. Rump Cap	13. Flank
4. Short Loin	9. Round	
5. Sirloin	10. Brisket	

1. Head	5. Loin/ Tenderloin	9. Ribs
2. Clear Plate	6. Ham	10. Bacon/Belly
3. Back Fat	7. Cheek	11. Hock
4. Boston Butt / Shoulder	8. Picnic Shoulder	

PERENNIAL FAVORITES

FOOD	TEMP	TIME	INTERNAL TEMP	WOOD
2-inch steak (rare)	500°F	10 minutes per side	135°F	Hickory
2-inch steak (medium)	500°F	12 minutes per side	145°F	Hickory
2-inch steak (well)	500°F	15 minutes per side	155°F	Hickory
Brisket	225°F	14–18 hours	190°F	Hickory or mesquite
Tri-tip (medium)	375°F	45 minutes	145°F	Mesquite
Whole chicken	375°F	80 minutes	170°F	Oak
Chicken breasts	325°F	35 minutes	170°F	Maple
Chicken wings	375°F	20 minutes	170°F	Oak or maple
Pork tenderloin	180°F	2–4 hours	145°F	Apple
Pork chops	375°F	10 minutes per side	145°F	Apple or pecan
Bacon	300°F	20 minutes	N/A	Apple
Pulled pork	225°F	16–18 hours	203°F	Hickory or apple
½-inch salmon fillet	325°F	25 minutes	145°F	Alder
Shrimp kebabs	375°F	6 minutes per side	N/A	Alder
Lobster tails	400°F	20 minutes	145°F	Alder
Ears of corn	400°F	25 minutes	N/A	Hickory or alder
⅛-inch potato wedges	375°F	45 minutes	N/A	Alder
Grilled asparagus	325°F	10 minutes	N/A	Hickory
Smoked hard-boiled eggs	180°F	30 minutes	N/A	Hickory
Smoked cheese crackers	180°F	30 minutes, flip, then 30 more minutes	N/A	Hickory or mesquite

'Cue Pals

When cooking on your pellet grill, as with anything else, you'll find that you have go-to items in the kitchen that you'll need on the regular. They can range from basic salt and pepper to your favorite mustard or local artisan honey. Here, I'll let you in on some of my kitchen favorites. A lot of these are my must-haves, and I go through them quickly. All of them will be used multiple times in this book.

Pantry Essentials

Salt and pepper: Many of the world's best grillers use only salt and pepper for seasoning to let the meat and wood flavor come through.

Garlic powder: For the rest of us who aren't world elites, a few simple spices can go a long way. Garlic powder is where my collection begins, and it does a lot of heavy lifting to bring out a ton of flavor.

Dillweed: As you will discover, I am a huge seafood fan. Dillweed is a must-have for seafood grilling.

Onion powder: Onion powder is another basic spice that will serve a purpose in many of the cooks in this book as a part of my arsenal of simple rubs, sauces, and marinades.

Brown sugar: Yes, I sing the Rolling Stones song every time I pull it from the pantry. Brown sugar is a must-have for pork as well as baking, and you'll find it's nearly ubiquitous in the sauces and rubs in chapter 9.

Local honey: It doesn't *have* to be local, but it's worth investing in the stuff that tastes really good. Plus, you should always support your local businesses whenever possible.

Olive oil: I use this as a sealer for my cast iron, and it's often the first thing I put on poultry, even before salt and pepper. I also sometimes use it in place of butter.

Refrigerator Essentials

Yellow mustard: Many of my cooks start with a simple rub of yellow mustard. If mustard is not something that you're already using all the time at the grill, it will be now that you have this book.

Barbecue sauce: Find a barbecue sauce you like and keep it around—I personally like Five Monkeys. Of course, you can always try my own recipe, Slightly Spicy Barbecue Sauce (page 145), but it's worth shopping around and trying different combos to find your favorite flavors.

Soy sauce: This is a must-have for marinades, providing earthiness that will punch up the flavor of almost any meat or vegetable.

Worcestershire sauce: Another necessity for marinades and more, you'll find this sauce used in several recipes in this book. It provides a complexity of flavor that's hard to substitute with something else.

Maple syrup: I mostly use this for pork, but I reach for it often enough that it's well worth keeping on hand.

Butter: Butter is used all over the place in pellet grilling. I especially love using it as a baster for poultry, even though I feel my cholesterol going up as I do it.

Soda: I've always loved Pepsi, and I typically have it on hand. A great griller once told me he wraps his ribs with Mountain Dew because it's his and his brother's favorite. Well, I like Pepsi, so there you have it—but feel free to use whatever soda you're loyal to.

Golden Rules of Good Backyard Barbecue

Wash your hands: In a post–Covid-19 world, this should be fresh in everyone's mind. Plus, it's just respectful to yourself and those you are cooking for. This is especially important when handling raw meat. No one wants to get sick, and this is the easiest way to make sure that doesn't happen.

THE MORE THE MERRIER

One of the joys of pellet grilling is the ability to cook multiple items at the same time. Because of the generous, multilevel grill space that many pellet grills offer today, as well as the convection cooking, you can fill up your pellet grill however you like. Here are a few things to consider when grilling different items at the same time.

Make a plan: If you need to put different items on the grill at different times, a timer will be your friend. If you need to remove grill racks to make items fit, do it before the grill is piping hot. Get your tools ready and have them handy so you're not making a mad dash to the kitchen for a spatula before dinner burns.

Remember, not everything takes the same time: Though pellet grills allow you to cook multiple items at the same temperature, one may cook significantly faster than the other. Account for that during your planning—a few strips of bacon will cook up faster than a bunch of whole potatoes.

Watch out for drips: Most pellet grills these days come with a few tiered racks to allow for additional grilling space. Don't put something on the top that's greasy or will melt—it'll drip onto the foods below.

Watch the edges: You'll find that most pellet grills' hot spots are near the edges. The small space between the drain pan and the wall of the grill is where much of the heat escapes, and this area can get warmer than other parts of the grill. Be mindful of it when cooking, and you'll avoid any unexpected burns.

Beware stinky foods: Pungent-smelling foods, such as fish and other seafoods, shouldn't be cooked on the grill with baked goods or sweets, because there's always a chance the flavor will transfer and you'll end up with tuna-scented cinnamon rolls for dessert.

Always cook to temperature: Cooking by temperature, rather than strictly by time, will ensure that your meat is fully cooked but never dried out. I do provide time estimates in my recipes, but you should pay attention to the meat itself, not the clock. Time estimates will vary depending on where you live, the climate, and the time of day or year, but the temperature of the meat is something you can always count on for a consistent result.

Let your meat rest: The vast majority of grilled meats are not truly done until they've had time to rest. Many meats are still cooking when they're pulled off the grill, and we don't want to take away their chance to fully finish. Whenever applicable, I will provide you rest times for the recipes in this book, so don't skip them—you'll taste the difference.

Keep your tools nearby: Also known as the "Andrew is a lazy-***" rule. I hate walking back and forth to get my grilling tools, and I hate getting in trouble for it even more. Opening the door lets in the Oregon rain (or worse, the Arizona heat), and I've learned the hard way to keep what I need within arm's reach.

Sharpen your knives: Sharp knives will make your life so much easier. Whether for preparation or for slicing, using a sharp knife is much quicker and much safer than sawing through meat with a dull blade. If you're unsure how to sharpen a knife, there are plenty of services online that will take your knives and do the job for you—and a quality job at that!

Clean your grill: Let's face it: Barbecues and smokers produce grease, and grease can get gross. Take care of your grill regularly so it doesn't take on a life of its own. Clean the inside of your grill with a degreaser—I do so after every few bags of pellets I go through. And without a doubt, use disposable bucket and drain pan liners. Their convenience will save you hours of cleaning in the long run.

Store your pellets properly: Unless you're miraculously burning through multiple bags of pellets a week, I suggest investing in an airtight container (or two) for your pellets. As I mentioned earlier, moisture can wreak havoc on your pellets. Something as simple and cheap as a five-gallon bucket with a lid will protect your wood pellets so you don't have to frantically run outside to grab them at every chance of rain.

Check your pellets: You wouldn't just start your car and not look at the gas gauge, so don't do the same with your pellet grill. I can't tell you the number of cooks I've had to salvage (or flat-out ruined) because I walked away and forgot to refuel. On low-temperature cooks with slower burn times, I check my pellets every few hours. Don't lose out on an awesome meal because of something as simple as refilling the hopper.

Experiment and practice: This advice applies to the beginner and the expert alike. Practice is the most important thing you can do with your grill. You'll likely be disappointed in your first-ever brisket unless you follow a recipe and learn the techniques. Pick up some tips, consult a world-class Andrew Koster recipe, and try, try again.

Have fun: Probably the best part of pellet grilling is that it doesn't require you to spend all day tending a fire or laboring over the grill. Most of us grill for our friends and family, and we shouldn't have to sacrifice time with them in the name of great food. With a pellet grill, you don't have to give anything up—you can have a good time while also making an incredible meal.

The Recipes in This Book

The recipes in this book were chosen to give you a full understanding of how to use your grill. There's so much benefit to be gleaned from this versatile piece of equipment, and these recipes will give you a thorough crash course. There's an even split between easy recipes and more difficult ones, so you can learn the full capability of the pellet grill and gradually broaden your skill set. You may already be an expert in some other form of grilling or cooking, but I hope to open you up to a world where all of that can be done outside on a single piece of equipment with absolutely amazing results.

We'll touch upon recipes from several different cuisines in this book, which will show you your grill's versatility and how it blurs the lines of traditional barbecue. And we won't draw the line at meats and smoking—in the later chapters, you'll find recipes for veggies, sides, and desserts. We'll make sure to get down to the nitty-gritty in every recipe, with all details covered, including the basics of time and temperature and the specific type of wood pellet to use.

You'll also find different methods to try on the same cook, tips to make cooks easier or dress them up, and ideas to pair them with other dishes. We'll leave no stone unturned, ensuring you'll feel armed with a comprehensive knowledge of your pellet grill. After you get through this book, you'll be more than ready to wow your friends and family with all kinds of wood-fired goodness.

PART

Two

RECIPES

FOR YOUR

PELLET GRILL AND SMOKER

PELLET-GRILLED WHOLE CHICKEN ★ 36

POULTRY

POULTRY IS probably the protein I cook most often on the pellet grill. Since practically before I can remember, I've eaten pellet-grilled chicken as a regular part of my diet. Some of the things you'll find coming off my grill are chicken tenders, wings, drumsticks, and even the occasional whole turkey. In this chapter, we'll go over some of my favorite cuts and my time-tested ways to cook them, as well as some tricks to bring out a ton of flavor while retaining juiciness.

CUTS

Poultry is available at most grocery stores in a few different cuts: whole, breasts, tenders, wings, drums, and thighs. Chicken and turkey can typically be found in a grocery store's butcher case, cut into half- or quarter-bird portions. Most of us are used to chicken and turkey, but Cornish game hens, duck, quail, and other game birds are all great options, some of which you can likely find locally.

Many of the recipes that I come up with start from chicken. Chicken is a very inexpensive meat option, and you can cook it in a multitude of ways, so it's great for practicing your skills. Because turkey tends to be more expensive, I often practice my Thanksgiving recipe on a chicken so I can work out the kinks in my strategy before the big day.

TECHNIQUES

One of my favorite things about poultry is the variety of flavors you can get out of it—there are just so many different ways to prepare it on the grill. Each technique brings out something different. My current favorite ways are whole and skinless on the grill, but I don't stop there, since there are so many more ways to make amazing pellet-grilled poultry. From Maple-Smoked Turkey (page 37) to Cracker-Breaded Chicken Tenders (page 38) to Hot Duck! (page 45), there's something in this chapter for everybody.

At the supermarket, it's common to find whole birds prebrined or injected, turkeys especially. I am a serial injector, so I always check to make sure that the bird I'm injecting hasn't already been brined. Whole birds can also be spatchcocked, which is removing the breastbone and laying the body open flat on the grill.

You'll be introduced to many of the techniques I use to cook poultry in this chapter, but most important of all, I can't say enough good things about what a bit of smoking can do for flavor. I will regularly give most of my cooks a quick smoke before I turn the grill to a higher temperature, and that's especially true with poultry. When smoking and grilling, I do recommend you keep an eye out for cracking and breaking of the skin; to combat this,

I typically baste my birds with butter, but there are other ways to keep the skin intact and the meat inside juicy.

|||||||||||||||||||||||||||||||| **PRO TIPS** ||||||||||||||||||||||||||||||||||||||

→ On whole birds, make sure you apply the rub to the meat under the skin. This ensures that the rub can fully penetrate the meat for maximum flavor.

→ Inject and brine your birds whenever possible. If you're planning to cook poultry often, it's worth it to buy an injector. A bird's skin can act as a barrier, preventing the flavor of your seasoning from getting into the meat itself. Injecting and brining will push the flavors right into the meat.

→ If you like your wings separated (i.e., drumettes separate from flats), I recommend buying them that way from the store to save time. It's usually not too hard to find separated wings at the supermarket, and if you're a drumette snob like I am, you can even buy them by themselves.

→ Higher heat will work best to crisp up the skin on your poultry. If you want to get crispy skin, go to temperatures of 400°F and higher for best results.

Pellet-Grilled Whole Chicken

SERVES	PREP TIME	SMOKE TEMPERATURE
6 to 8	10 minutes	400°F

	SMOKE TIME	WOOD PELLET FLAVOR
	1½ hours	Hickory

CHICKEN IS A staple of the grilling world, and even more so in the realm of pellet grilling. Growing up in the shadow of the Traeger barn, I regularly saw barbe-cued chicken on our dinner table. Chicken was actually one of the ways that the word spread about the early pellet barbecues. Because chicken wasn't as common as the more traditional grilled hot dogs and hamburgers, whole chick-ens were frequently used for pellet-grilling demos, catering events, and other opportunities to showcase the great taste of pellet-grilled food. If you're new to pellet grilling, this is a great place to start, and it's still one of my favorites to this day.

1 whole chicken

2 batches Poultry Rub
(page 151)

1. Supply your smoker with wood pellets and follow the manufacturer's specific start-up procedure. Preheat the grill, with the lid closed, to 400°F.

2. Season the chicken with the rub, using your hands to ensure the seasoning is thoroughly rubbed into the skin.

3. Once the grill reaches 400°F, place the whole chicken directly on the grill. Cook until the internal temperature of the chicken reaches 170°F in the thickest part of the breast, about 1½ hours.

4. Once the internal temperature of the chicken breast reaches 170°F, remove the chicken from the grill. Let the whole bird rest for at least 15 minutes before carving and serving.

COOKING TIP: Leftover pellet-grilled chicken can be used in everything from sandwiches to soup. Here's one of our favorite ways of using day-old chicken: First, we cut all the meat off the bones, removing all the skin; then, we use meat claws to shred the chicken meat. I throw all that shredded chicken right in a cast-iron skillet with some spices for a quick taco filling.

Maple-Smoked Turkey

SERVES	PREP TIME	SMOKE TEMPERATURE
10 to 14	25 minutes	180°F, then 350°F
	SMOKE TIME	WOOD PELLET FLAVOR
	3 to 4 hours	Maple

EVER SINCE I was young, I've looked forward to my dad's smoked turkey. I've carried on the tradition, and I don't know how many turkeys I have smoked in my lifetime, but I know it's a lot—from Thanksgiving to practicing-for-Thanksgiving to teaching turkey prep to getting a random wild idea in the middle of the summer. We've all had bone-dry, inedible turkey, so I'm going to make sure you don't do that to your family. The key to the perfect turkey is to avoid overcooking it—pulling it off the grill right at 170°F will ensure the moistest turkey you've ever had.

1 batch Butter Poultry
Injectable (page 148)

1 whole turkey

2 tablespoons olive oil

2 batches Poultry Rub
(page 151)

1. Supply your smoker with wood pellets and follow the manufacturer's specific start-up procedure. Preheat the grill, with the lid closed, and set to smoke mode or 180°F.

2. Using an injector, inject the breasts and legs of the turkey with the poultry injectable.

3. Coat the turkey with the olive oil all over, then season it with the rub, using your hands to ensure you work the seasoning into the skin.

4. Place the whole turkey directly on the grill grate and allow it to smoke for 2½ hours.

5. After 2½ hours, increase the grill temperature to 350°F. Allow the turkey to continue cooking until its internal temperature reaches 170°F in the thickest part of the breast, around 1½ hours longer. Keep an eye on it as time goes on so you can make sure you avoid overcooking.

6. As soon as the turkey's internal temperature hits 170°F, remove it from the grill. Let it rest for at least 15 minutes before carving and serving.

Cracker-Breaded Chicken Tenders

SERVES	PREP TIME	SMOKE TEMPERATURE
3 to 5	10 minutes	350°F

	SMOKE TIME	WOOD PELLET FLAVOR
	25 minutes	Alder

CHICKEN TENDERS ARE a go-to in my home. With three kids who are always on the move, we often choose this for a quick and tasty meal. To avoid falling into a rut, we make our tenders in all sorts of ways—everything from sauce glazed to Cajun to teriyaki. To this day, though, my favorite way to make tenders is breading them—I can't resist the texture, and I appreciate the extra flavor. Years ago, my mom showed me how to bread chicken tenders with Triscuits. I've seen other, similar methods over the years, but this way continues to produce the best results in terms of flavor and texture.

1 batch Poultry Rub (page 151), or your favorite chicken seasoning

⅓ cup flour

1 large egg, beaten

½ box shredded wheat crackers, crushed (I prefer Triscuit brand)

1 pound boneless, skinless chicken breast tenders

1. Supply your smoker with wood pellets and follow the manufacturer's specific start-up procedure. Preheat the grill, with the lid closed, to 350°F.

2. In a small, shallow bowl or pan, combine the rub with the flour. Crack the egg into a separate shallow bowl and whisk thoroughly. Pour the crushed crackers into a third shallow dish. You'll use these three mixtures to dredge the tenders.

3. To dredge the tenders, dip them first in the flour mixture, then the egg, and finally the crushed crackers. Give each tender a quick shake after dipping to prevent excess breading. Set the breaded tenders on a plate or tray for easy access.

4. Once the grill has reached 350°F, gently place the tenders directly on the grill grate to cook. Cook the tenders until they reach an internal temperature of 170°F, about 25 minutes. Remove from the grill and serve immediately.

Teriyaki Chicken Skewers

SERVES	PREP TIME	SMOKE TEMPERATURE
3 to 5	15 minutes	300°F

	SMOKE TIME	WOOD PELLET FLAVOR
	25 minutes	Pecan

THIS ONE IS for the kiddos. Teriyaki is one of my kids' favorite flavors, and they're not alone. I love teriyaki chicken, but kids and adults alike know that a skewer makes everything more fun to eat. If you're looking for something to grill at your next barbecue that's a guaranteed crowd favorite, look no further—this easy recipe is the one for you.

1 pound boneless, skinless chicken breast tenders

1 batch Poultry Rub (page 151)

1 batch Teriyaki Sauce (page 146)

1. Supply your smoker with wood pellets and follow the manufacturer's specific start-up procedure. Preheat the grill, with the lid closed, to 300°F.

2. Season the cut chicken breast tenders with the rub, using your hands to work the seasoning into the chicken.

3. Thread each seasoned chicken tender vertically onto a presoaked wood skewer, leaving 2 to 3 inches of empty space on either end.

4. Once the grill reaches 300°F, place the skewers directly on the grill and cook them until the internal temperature of the chicken reaches 170°F, 20 to 25 minutes. (This is a good time to throw together the teriyaki sauce, if necessary.)

5. Once the chicken is cooked through, use a basting brush to baste the skewers on both sides with the teriyaki sauce and cook for 2 more minutes. Remove the skewers from the grill and serve immediately.

COOKING TIP: Teriyaki skewers make a showstopping appetizer. Grill up some skewers before your next party and have them ready for the guests to gobble up while you wait for the ribs.

Buffalo Wings

SERVES	PREP TIME	SMOKE TEMPERATURE
6 to 8	5 minutes	400°F
	SMOKE TIME	WOOD PELLET FLAVOR
	25 minutes	Alder

I LOVE ALL sports. And while baseball in particular has given me some of my greatest sports moments, deep down, I'm all about the pigskin. My all-time favorite food during football season is buffalo wings. And I'm not talking about some sweet, churched-up version; I'm talking about unadulterated garlic, vinegar, and spice. Now, the last thing I want to do when my OSU Beavers are up on a Saturday night is spend all evening babysitting the grill, working on the wings, so this is my low-maintenance take on buffalo wings. It's an easy and quick way to get the same classic game-day favorite on your pellet grill.

1 pound split
   chicken wings

1 batch Blackened Cajun
   Rub (page 152)

1 cup vinegar-based
   hot sauce (I like
   Frank's RedHot)

Bleu cheese or ranch
   dressing, for serving

Carrot sticks, for serving

Celery sticks, for serving

1. Supply your smoker with wood pellets and follow the manufacturer's specific start-up procedure. Preheat the grill, with the lid closed, to 400°F.

2. In a large mixing bowl, season the chicken wings with the rub. Toss to coat.

3. Once the grill reaches 400°F, place the chicken wings directly on the grill grate. Cook until the internal temperature of the wings reaches 170°F, about 25 minutes.

4. Remove the wings, transfer them to a second large mixing bowl, and douse them with the hot sauce. Toss the wings to thoroughly cover them with sauce.

5. Serve the wings with bleu cheese or ranch for dipping, with a side of carrots and celery.

COOKING TIP: If your pellet grill gives you the ability to cook over an open flame, this is the time to use it. The direct heat from the fire will give your wings a lot more of the char that you might be used to on a gas or charcoal grill—and, of course, the char tastes great.

Roast Turkey Breast

SERVES	PREP TIME	SMOKE TEMPERATURE
2 to 4	10 minutes	350°F

	SMOKE TIME	WOOD PELLET FLAVOR
	1 hour	Apple

ONE BIG REASON that we reserve turkey for a few special occasions throughout the year is that cooking a full bird leaves our family with weeks' worth of leftovers. Most times of the year a full turkey is just too much, so when you're in the mood for turkey but a full bird isn't an option, turkey breast is where it's at! I often pick up a turkey breast on my way home from work and give it a quick cook on the grill. Roast turkey breast is a perfect meal for your family, and you won't be stuck with a picked-over turkey carcass sitting for days on end in your refrigerator.

1 (4-pound) turkey breast

1 tablespoon olive oil

1 batch Poultry Rub (page 151)

1. Supply your smoker with wood pellets and follow the manufacturer's specific start-up procedure. Preheat the grill, with the lid closed, to 350°F.

2. Coat the turkey breast with olive oil all over. Season it with the rub, using your hands to rub the seasoning into and under the skin.

3. Place the turkey breast directly on the grill grate and cook until the internal temperature reaches 170°F in the thickest part of the breast, about 1 hour.

4. When the turkey reaches temperature, remove it from the heat and slice. Serve hot.

COOKING TIP: If you want to give your turkey breast a bit of extra-smoky flavor, you can cook it on the smoke setting for 1 hour, then crank the temperature up to 350°F to finish it, until the internal temperature reaches 170°F.

Too-Sweet Chicken Lollipops

SERVES	PREP TIME	SMOKE TEMPERATURE
2 to 4	15 minutes	400°F, then 300°F

	SMOKE TIME	WOOD PELLET FLAVOR
	25 minutes	Hickory

DRUMSTICKS ARE ALWAYS a crowd pleaser, and that's why they're one of my favorite items to bring to a party. Not only are they relatively cheap and easy to make, but I also feel like the life of the party whenever I arrive with a Tupperware full of on-the-bone protein instead of the more standard chips and guac. Making drumstick "lollipops" is a great way to change things up. To make drumsticks into lollipops, cut the skin from the bottom of the drumstick off the bone, leaving the meat. For this recipe, we'll also add a little of my Slightly Spicy Barbecue Sauce (page 145) for a punch of sweetness and spice to boot.

1 pound chicken drumsticks

1 batch Sweet and Spicy Rub (page 154)

½ cup Slightly Spicy Barbecue Sauce (page 145)

1. Supply your smoker with wood pellets and follow the manufacturer's specific start-up procedure. Preheat the grill, with the lid closed, to 400°F.

2. Using kitchen shears, cut through the chicken skin and tendons just below the meaty area of the drumstick. Cut all the way around the drumstick, then remove the bottom portion of skin and discard. The bone should be exposed, leaving a "lollipop" of meat at the top.

3. Season the meat of the drumsticks with the sweet and spicy rub, using your hands to rub it thoroughly into the skin.

4. Place the drumsticks directly on the grill grate. Cook until their internal temperature reaches 170°F, 15 to 20 minutes.

5. Once the chicken reaches temperature, reduce the grill temperature to 300°F. Using a basting brush, brush the drumstick meat with the barbecue sauce, keeping them on the grill throughout.

6. Cook the brushed drumsticks for 7 additional minutes, until the sauce is somewhat caramelized. Remove the drumsticks from the grill and serve hot.

COOKING TIP: A leg and wing grill rack is an awesome tool to have on hand for this cook. Hanging your drumsticks will allow you to get more in the grill and will ensure the lollipops are cooked evenly all the way through. Most barbecue retailers sell a chicken leg hanger of some kind, so if you cook drumsticks a lot, it's definitely the right investment for you.

Smoked Cornish Game Hens

SERVES	PREP TIME	SMOKE TEMPERATURE
2 to 4	10 minutes	180°F, then 350°F
	SMOKE TIME	WOOD PELLET FLAVOR
	1 hour 30 minutes	Alder

CORNISH GAME HENS are something I hadn't tried until a bit later in life. I spent my college years working at a grocery store, so I was aware of what they were, but I never thought to try them until my wife brought them home years later. When I did get a taste, I immediately understood why they were so popular at the store all those years—they're just darn good. Cornish game hens pack a lot of flavor in a smaller package. They are popular in the United Kingdom, and their small size makes them an ideal dish for couples or singles. Add a side of Barbecued Roasted Potatoes (page 114), and you have yourself an easy pellet-grill meal.

2 whole Cornish game hens

2 tablespoons olive oil

1 batch Poultry Rub (page 151)

1. Supply your smoker with wood pellets and follow the manufacturer's specific start-up procedure. Preheat the grill, with the lid closed, to 180°F.

2. Coat the hens with olive oil all over, then season with the rub, using your hands to thoroughly rub the seasoning into the skin.

3. Once the grill reaches 180°F, place the hens directly on the grill grate and allow them to smoke for 45 minutes.

4. After 45 minutes, increase the grill's temperature to 350°F. Continue cooking the hens until their internal temperature reaches 170°F in the thickest part of the breast, another 30 to 45 minutes.

5. Once they're cooked through, remove the hens from the grill and serve immediately.

COOKING TIP: They sound fancy, but Cornish game hens are actually a hit with kids! We like to buy each of our children a hen for dinner–it's fun for them to have a bird to themselves. Of course, they never finish it, but it gives us leftovers for sandwiches or pasta the next day.

Hot Duck!

SERVES	PREP TIME	SMOKE TEMPERATURE
6 to 8	20 minutes	375°F
	SMOKE TIME	WOOD PELLET FLAVOR
	1½ hours	Hickory

DUCK ISN'T A regular item on our table, but it really should be. My favorite thing about duck is that it is basically all dark meat, which means exponentially more flavor. I've found using an injectable packs the poultry full of flavor to rock the entire table's taste buds. (Of course, the rival of my beloved Oregon State Beavers is the Oregon Ducks, so my precision with cooking duck is a bit of a lighthearted dig.) Along with the injectable, this recipe uses my spicy Blackened Cajun Rub (page 152) to bring the flavor over the top.

1 (5.5-pound) whole duck

1 batch Butter Poultry Injectable (page 148)

2 tablespoons olive oil

2 batches Blackened Cajun Rub (page 152)

1. Supply your smoker with wood pellets and follow the manufacturer's specific start-up procedure. Preheat the grill, with the lid closed, to 375°F.

2. Use an injector to inject the breasts and legs of the duck with the poultry injectable.

3. Coat the duck all over with the olive oil, and then season it with the rub, using your hands to work the rub into the skin.

4. Once the grill reaches 375°F, place the duck directly on the grill grate. Cook the duck until its internal temperature reaches 170°F in the thickest part of the breast, about 1½ hours.

5. Once it's cooked through, remove the duck from the grill, carve, and serve.

COOKING TIP: Whole poultry is where your grill combo tool can come in especially handy. When cooking whole duck, chicken, and even turkey, I always use my tongs-spatula combo tool. It allows me to get underneath the duck with the spatula while still gripping it with the tongs, giving me the flexibility I need while grilling.

Brenna's Turkey Pot Pie

SERVES	PREP TIME	SMOKE TEMPERATURE
6	40 minutes	425°F
	SMOKE TIME	WOOD PELLET FLAVOR
	35 minutes	Alder

LAST WINTER. my wife and I visited our close friends Wade and Brenna, and Brenna made the absolute best pot pie of all time. I had never been a fan of pot pie before, and I hadn't even eaten one since childhood, but it was one of the best meals I had ever had. This is my take on Brenna's pot pie, and you know I couldn't resist moving it to the grill. I think the added wood-fired flavor only makes this already-amazing dish even better.

½ cup (1 stick) butter

½ cup flour

½ cup finely diced onion

½ teaspoon salt

¼ teaspoon freshly ground black pepper

2 cups chicken broth

½ cup milk

3 cups Roast Turkey Breast (page 41), cut into bite-size pieces

1 cup frozen peas

1 cup frozen carrots

1 (14-ounce) package store-bought refrigerated pie crusts, softened per package directions

Malt vinegar, for serving

1. Set a cast-iron or other all-purpose saucepan directly on the grill. Supply your smoker with wood pellets and follow the manufacturer's specific start-up procedure. Preheat the grill, with the lid closed, to 425°F.

2. Once the grill has reached 425°F, put the butter in the saucepan and allow it to melt. Once melted, whisk in the flour, onion, salt, and pepper. Cook, stirring constantly, until the mixture is bubbly, then remove it from the heat.

3. Stir the chicken broth and milk into the saucepan and heat the mixture until boiling, stirring constantly. Allow the mixture to boil for 1 minute, stirring continuously.

4. Stir in the roasted turkey breast, peas, and carrots. Remove the mixture from the grill.

5. Roll 1 pie crust into a 13-inch round and transfer it to a 9-inch pie tin. Pour the pie filling mixture into the crust-lined tin.

6. Roll the remaining pie crust into an 11-inch round and center it on top of the pie filling. Turn the crust edges under and crimp them with the tines of a fork to create a seal. Use a knife to make a few air vents in the top pie crust.

7. Place the pie directly on the grill grate and bake it for 35 minutes, or until it is golden brown on top. Let the pie sit for about 15 minutes to allow the filling to thicken. Serve with malt vinegar.

COOKING TIP: To give your pie a more golden finish, brush the top crust with a 50-50 mixture of beaten egg and water just before baking on the grill.

SWEET AND SPICY BABY BACKS ★ 54

PORK

I COULD GENUINELY eat pork for days on end with not much else on the menu. Pork has a mild but still plenty meaty flavor that works well with so many ingredients, especially spicy and sweet combinations. With a wide array of cuts that you can prepare in countless different ways, pork is a very versatile meat. Low and slow is the most popular way to cook pork—that's how we get ribs, pork shoulders, and other cuts that practically melt in your mouth after bathing in a long smoke. That fall-off-the-bone, pull-apart meat is what many of us are looking for when a pork craving hits. Fortunately, this is easy to achieve with your pellet grill.

CUTS

Pork is available at your local grocery store's butcher case in a wide variety of cuts. Pork shoulders, ham, loins, and ribs are some of the popular options. Ribs are my favorite, with the most popular options being baby backs and spareribs. Baby backs are the leaner meat, coming from the back, while spareribs are the fattier ribs from the underside of the pig. Pork shoulders and ham are also two distinct cuts, with pork shoulder and "pork butt" coming from the front of the pig—the latter ironically so—while the ham is located on the backside. Ham is sometimes sold uncooked ("fresh"), but it's more commonly available precooked, so know what you're after when you head to the butcher. Loins, pork chops, and belly are also two commonly used parts of the pig. Loins and pork chops come from the back of the pig, and pork belly comes from the pig's underside, known to most of us in its cured form as bacon.

TECHNIQUES

The technique we use most commonly with pork is low and slow. As I've mentioned previously, low and slow is the method of smoking at low temperatures for a long period of time. This is the technique used to produce pulled pork, fall-apart ribs, bacon, and many other barbecue favorites.

Low and slow might be the most commonly associated with pork, but that isn't to say that there aren't other methods of grilling pork, such as roasting and searing, that don't produce equally amazing results. In reality, one of the great things about pork is that there are so many ways to cook it. For instance, when working with pork chops, grilling and searing (rather than smoking) is ideal—see Classic Pork Chops (page 66). I have also found myself reverse-searing cuts for a nice charred crust, like in Smoked and Seared Pork Tenderloins (page 56).

Meats like sausages and bacon are typically grilled, but that doesn't mean you can't smoke your bacon or braise your sausage. If you pick up a precooked ham at the grocery store, you'll want to roast it on the grill to bring it to temp, but including a little pellet smoke to start the cook will make all the difference in the world. I also often braise my pork roasts, throwing them on the grill with some broth and vegetables in a cast-iron skillet. As you get more comfortable working with your pellet grill, you'll see the innumerable possibilities that await you when it comes to cooking pork.

→ When wrapping meat, butcher paper can be used as a substitute for aluminum foil in most cases. I wouldn't suggest using paper if you're going to be adding other liquids to the cook (since liquid will leak out of paper), but as long as you're not adding liquid, it should work great.

→ If you're worried about the meat getting dry during a long smoke, inject your pork shoulders. Injecting pork shoulders will add more flavor and help keep the meat moist, even though that typically isn't much of a problem on a pellet grill.

→ Experiment with natural sweeteners. Pork goes great with sweet flavors, and some of the best ones are maple syrup and apple juice. Both of these are great ingredients to use for injecting, basting, and braising.

→ For the best bark (which is that delicious, flavor-packed crust around the outside) on your meat, avoid using pans. If you're cooking a pork shoulder or something similar and want the most bark, you should aim to give the meat as much direct contact with the smoke for as long as humanly possible.

Pulled Pork Barbecue Sandwiches

SERVES	PREP TIME	SMOKE TEMPERATURE
8	15 minutes for pork, 10 for sandwiches	225°F
	SMOKE TIME	WOOD PELLET FLAVOR
	16 to 20 hours	Hickory

I CAN'T COUNT how many pork shoulders I've cooked over the years—the number just keeps going up and up. I've cooked them for countless meals, but I also frequently use them in a professional capacity to test grills. There are unique challenges that pork shoulders pose for pellet grills: They're big, they need to be cooked low and slow, and, of course, they produce a lot of grease, so they're good for testing a grill's limits. With that said, a good pellet grill can do wonders to a pork shoulder. One crowd favorite is this classic.

FOR THE PULLED PORK

1 (6 to 8 pound) bone-in pork shoulder

2 tablespoons yellow mustard

2 batches Pork Rub (page 150)

FOR THE SANDWICHES

8 brioche buns

1 cup Slightly Spicy Barbecue Sauce (2 tablespoons per sandwich) (page 145)

2 cups sauerkraut (¼ cup per sandwich) (I like Cleveland Kitchen brand's Gnar Gnar Spicy Sauerkraut)

TO MAKE THE PULLED PORK

1. Rub the whole pork shoulder with the mustard, then season with the pork rub, using your hands to rub the seasonings into the meat.

2. Supply your smoker with wood pellets and follow the manufacturer's specific start-up procedure. Preheat the grill, with the lid closed, to 225°F.

3. Once the grill reaches 225°F, place the meat directly on the grill. Smoke the pork shoulder until its internal temperature reaches 203°F. Note that this is a low-and-slow smoke, upwards of 16 hours.

4. Once it reaches temperature, pull the pork shoulder from the grill and set it aside to rest. Rest time can be up to around 1 hour, until the meat is tender enough that you can pull the pork apart by hand. Remove the shoulder bone and pull the pork apart, using only your fingers.

TO MAKE THE SANDWICHES

5. Set out the brioche buns. Spoon ½ cup of pulled pork on each bottom bun, followed by 2 tablespoons of barbecue sauce and ¼ cup of sauerkraut. Top with the remaining buns and serve immediately.

COOKING TIP: Pulled pork sandwich condiments and toppings can really be whatever your heart desires. My wife and I love to throw on a generous dollop of horseradish, and I also like to add spicy mustard and mayonnaise. Try swapping out the sauerkraut for pickle chips or another favorite of mine, pepperoncini.

Sweet and Spicy Baby Backs

SERVES 4 to 6	PREP TIME 25 minutes	SMOKE TEMPERATURE 180°F, then 350°F
	SMOKE TIME 4 hours	WOOD PELLET FLAVOR Apple

BABY BACK RIBS might just be my forte. I know tri-tip might have something to say about that, but I'll leave them for later. I started working on perfecting baby backs when I was in college. I'd invite my friends over for barbecues during our all-too-short Northwest summers, and I would make ribs almost every time. Recently, my oldest daughter has taken a liking to ribs, so now I cook them quite often for her. This prized recipe, developed over many years, combines all the elements that make for a great rib: spiciness, sweetness, and smoke. The flavor combination is perfect, and along with the technique, this recipe will give you amazingly delicious and tender ribs every time.

2 (2- to 3-pound) racks baby back ribs

2 tablespoons yellow mustard

1 batch Sweet and Spicy Rub (page 154)

2 tablespoons brown sugar

1 cup Pepsi or other soda

¼ cup Slightly Spicy Barbecue Sauce (page 145)

1. Remove the membrane from the back of the ribs by cutting through the membrane in an X pattern. Use a paper towel to grip the membrane to help pull it off.

2. Supply your smoker with wood pellets and follow the manufacturer's specific start-up procedure. Preheat the grill, with the lid closed, to 180°F.

3. Massage the ribs with the mustard, followed by the rub. Use your hands to thoroughly work the rub into the ribs.

4. Once the grill reaches 180°F, place the ribs directly on the grill grate. Smoke the ribs for 3 hours.

5. After 3 hours, remove the ribs from the grill and put them on enough aluminum foil to allow you to wrap them up completely in the next step. Sprinkle the brown sugar on the ribs.

6. Fold up the bottom of the foil, then fold in the two sides. Fold the top up enough to protect liquid from escaping, but leave an opening to add the soda. Pour in the soda, then fold the top of the aluminum foil closed, enclosing the ribs and the liquid.

7. Return the wrapped ribs to the grill. Increase the grill's temperature to 350°F, and continue to cook the ribs for 45 more minutes. (This is a good time to make the barbecue sauce, if necessary.)

8. After 45 minutes, remove the ribs from the aluminum foil. Using a basting brush, brush the ribs with the barbecue sauce.

9. Return the ribs to the grill and cook them for 10 more minutes. Then, remove the racks of ribs from the grill, cut them into individual ribs, and serve immediately.

COOKING TIP: If time allows, you can prep your ribs (steps 1 and 3) anywhere from a couple of hours to a day before cooking. Allowing more time will give the rub a chance to penetrate the meat, making for an even better flavor post-grill.

Smoked and Seared Pork Tenderloins

SERVES	PREP TIME	SMOKE TEMPERATURE
4 to 6	15 minutes	180°F, then 500°F
	SMOKE TIME	WOOD PELLET FLAVOR
	2 to 3 hours	Maple

AT MY HOUSE. cooking pork tenderloin is a regular occurrence. They're one of the easiest meats to cook on the grill—you can really just set them on the grill and let them go until they reach temperature—but I'm always looking to change the style up a bit. After trying all kinds of marinades, sauces, and the like, I wanted to try something new mid-smoke, so I moved the tenderloins aside, opened my pellet grill's flame broiler, and gave the tenderloins the reverse-searing treatment. The char added a better, deeper flavor to the tenderloins, and there weren't any leftovers.

2 (1-pound)
  pork tenderloins

1 batch Pork Rub
  (page 150)

1. Generously season the tenderloins with the rub, using your hands to ensure the rub thoroughly coats the meat. Place the tenderloins directly on the grill grate (yes, you can do this before preheating).

2. Supply your smoker with wood pellets and follow the manufacturer's specific start-up procedure. Preheat the grill, with the lid closed, to 180°F.

3. Allow the tenderloins to smoke for 2 hours, or until their internal temperature reaches 125°F.

4. After 2 hours, increase the grill temperature to 500°F (or, if applicable, turn on your grill's open flame). Sear the tenderloins on either side, about 10 minutes each, until their internal temperature reaches 145°F.

5. Remove the seared tenderloins from the grill and allow them to rest for 10 minutes before thinly slicing and serving.

COOKING TIP: Another way to sear your tenderloins is in a cast-iron skillet. Place your skillet directly on the grill, set the grill to 400°F, and add a couple of tablespoons of butter to the pan. Once the butter melts, add the tenderloins and sear for about 10 minutes per side, or until they reach an internal temperature of 145°F.

BLTA

SERVES	PREP TIME	SMOKE TEMPERATURE
2	5 minutes	300°F
	SMOKE TIME	WOOD PELLET FLAVOR
	25 minutes	Hickory

THERE AREN'T MANY better things on this planet than a BLT, so there's no way to make it better, right? That's what I thought, but I was mistaken, and it turns out few slices of avocado make all the difference. I had my first experience with a BLTA at a bar in my hometown years ago. Ever since then, every time I have a BLT, I feel like there's something missing. But it turns out even a BLTA can be taken to an even better level by—you guessed it—throwing the bacon on the pellet grill.

1 pound PG Bacon (page 58)

4 slices sourdough, or your favorite bread

Mayonnaise to taste

1 avocado

1 tomato

2 large lettuce leaves

1. Supply your smoker with wood pellets and follow the manufacturer's specific start-up procedure. Preheat the grill, with the lid closed, to 300°F.

2. Place the bacon and sliced bread directly on the grill grate, making sure the bacon doesn't reach past the area covered by the drain pan.

3. After 3 minutes, remove the bread from the grill. Coat one side of each slice with mayonnaise and set aside.

4. Continue smoking the bacon for 20 minutes, or until it reaches your desired crispiness. Meanwhile, slice the avocado and tomato and set aside.

5. Remove the bacon from the grill and put it directly onto two of the slices of bread. Top the sandwiches with the tomato, avocado, lettuce, and remaining bread. Serve immediately.

COOKING TIP: For extra-smoky flavor, you can also smoke the avocado. Cut the avocados in half, remove the pits, peel off the skins, and smoke them at 180°F for 20 minutes.

PG Bacon

SERVES	PREP TIME	SMOKE TEMPERATURE
8 to 10	15 minutes, plus 8 to 10 days curing	180°F
	SMOKE TIME	WOOD PELLET FLAVOR
	3 to 4 hours	Maple

I KNOW I'VE said a lot of things are done better on the pellet grill, but I have to say it again: It's impossible to beat home-smoked bacon. I love store-bought bacon as much as the next guy, but making your own bacon brings it to a whole new plane of flavor. This recipe will give you an amazing peppered bacon that you can slice to your own desired thickness, perfect for Sunday breakfast or an afternoon BLT. Note that the pork belly needs to cure for 8 to 10 days, so plan accordingly for when you want to enjoy your bacon.

⅓ cup kosher salt

½ cup packed brown sugar

2½ tablespoons freshly ground black pepper

½ teaspoon curing salt

3 pounds pork belly, skin removed

1. In a small bowl, mix together the dry ingredients: kosher salt, brown sugar, pepper, and curing salt.

2. Season the pork belly with the dry mixture, using your hands to rub it into the meat.

3. Put the seasoned pork belly in a gallon-size resealable plastic bag. Leave it in the refrigerator to cure for 8 to 10 days.

4. When you're ready to smoke, supply your smoker with wood pellets and follow the manufacturer's specific start-up procedure. Preheat the grill, with the lid closed, and set to smoke mode or 180°F.

5. Remove the cured pork belly from the plastic bag, rinse it under cold water, and pat it dry with paper towels.

6. Place the cured pork belly directly on the grill grate. Smoke it until the internal temperature reaches 150°F, usually between 3 and 4 hours. Remove the pork belly from the grill and slice it into strips of bacon, adjusting the thickness to your preference.

Hardwood Ham

SERVES 8 to 10	**PREP TIME** 15 minutes	**SMOKE TEMPERATURE** 350°F
	SMOKE TIME 3 to 4 hours	**WOOD PELLET FLAVOR** Hickory

THERE WAS A time when I saw ham as the undesirable lunch meat I got when the turkey ran out. I never loved ham sandwiches, and the precooked ham from the supermarket that we had every Easter wasn't much better. When I got older and started working for Traeger Grills, I learned of the spectacular treat that is fresh-smoked ham. There's a reason ham is a classic holiday staple—a well-cooked ham is *really* good. Ham can be an easy, high-payoff cook on a pellet grill, and trying this recipe just one time will make you forget all about every mediocre precooked spiral ham you suffered through for so many years.

1 (14- to 16-pound) fresh ham

4 garlic cloves, thinly sliced

2 tablespoons olive oil

Salt

Freshly ground black pepper

1. Supply your smoker with wood pellets and follow the manufacturer's specific start-up procedure. Preheat the grill, with the lid closed, to 350°F.

2. Use a stiff boning knife to slice a 1-inch crosshatch pattern into the skin of the ham, being careful not to cut into the meat.

3. Insert slices of garlic into the intersections of the crosshatched skin of the ham. Rub the ham with olive oil, then season it with salt and pepper.

4. Once the grill reaches 350°F, place the ham directly on the grill grate. Roast the ham until its internal temperature reaches 145°F, roughly 3 hours, but up to 4 hours depending on size.

5. Once the ham is cooked through, remove it from the grill and slice. Serve hot.

COOKING TIP: Glazes are great for fresh ham (just like for precooked ham). If you're applying a glaze, use an aluminum pan to catch the drippings so you don't end up glazing your entire grill. Honey makes a great glaze, and there are fantastic store-bought options as well.

Ham and Potato Hash

SERVES 4 to 6	PREP TIME 15 minutes	SMOKE TEMPERATURE 400°F
	SMOKE TIME 25 minutes	WOOD PELLET FLAVOR Oak

MAKING A FULL meal in a hurry can be difficult—often, it involves running in and out of the house, tending to multiple appliances, and at the end leaving a mess. To make things easier, I'm always trying to finagle creating an entire meal using just one appliance, as well as one knife, one cutting board, one cooking utensil, and so on. This ham and potato hash falls into the category of one-appliance meals, and it makes everything so much easier. This is one of my favorite easy meals, and you'll see why. I use a single cutting board and knife for the entire prep process, and then I throw everything in the skillet until done. It's so easy, super filling, and tastes very good.

5 medium red potatoes

2 bell peppers

1 white onion

1 pound Hardwood Ham (page 59)

3 tablespoons olive oil

Salt

Freshly ground black pepper

1. Supply your smoker with wood pellets and follow the manufacturer's specific start-up procedure. Preheat the grill, with the lid closed, to 400°F.

2. Place the cast-iron skillet in the center of the grill.

3. Chop the ingredients in the order that you'll be putting them into the skillet: first the potatoes in 1-inch pieces, then the bell peppers in ½-inch chunks, and then the onion, finely diced. Finally, slice the ham in 1-inch cubes. Set everything aside so it's easy to access once it's time to grill.

4. Once the grill has reached 400°F, add the olive oil and potatoes to the skillet and cook for 5 minutes, stirring occasionally.

5. Add the bell peppers and stir them to incorporate. Add the onion and cook for 10 minutes, stirring occasionally.

6. Add the cubed ham and season with salt and pepper to taste. Continue cooking, stirring occasionally, until the potatoes and other veggies are tender. Remove the skillet from the heat and serve immediately.

COOKING TIP: I don't know about you, but to me, this dish screams "add cheese!" After serving myself a helping, I like to sprinkle a generous handful of cheddar cheese on top of my hash, and the dish should be hot enough so the cheese can melt on top of it right away.

Spicy Country Ribs

SERVES	PREP TIME	SMOKE TEMPERATURE
2 to 4	25 minutes	180°F, then 350°F

	SMOKE TIME	WOOD PELLET FLAVOR
	4½ hours	Apple

I LOVE COUNTRY ribs; they're packed full of flavor. Their name is somewhat misleading—the cut comes from the shoulder of the pig. You can find country ribs at almost any grocery store. Although they are cooked like baby backs, country ribs are their more tender but thicker cousin. My secret ingredient here is Pepsi, my personal favorite soda, but if for some reason you're a Coke devotee, I suppose you could use that instead.

2 pounds country-style ribs

2 tablespoons yellow mustard

1 batch Sweet and Spicy Rub (page 154)

2 tablespoons brown sugar

1 cup Pepsi or other soda

½ cup Slightly Spicy Barbecue Sauce (page 145)

1. Supply your smoker with wood pellets and follow the manufacturer's specific start-up procedure. Preheat the grill, with the lid closed, to 180°F.

2. Rub the ribs with mustard all over, then coat them with the rub, using your hands to ensure the seasoning is thoroughly rubbed into the meat.

3. Once the grill reaches 180°F, place the ribs directly on the grill grate and allow them to smoke for 3½ hours.

4. Remove the ribs from the grill. Put them on enough foil to wrap them up completely, then sprinkle them with the brown sugar.

5. Fold up the bottom of the foil, then fold in the two sides. Fold the top up enough to protect liquid from escaping, but leave an opening to add the soda. Pour in the soda, then fold the top of the aluminum foil closed, enclosing the ribs and the liquid.

6. Increase the grill's temperature to 350°F. Return the wrapped ribs to the grill and cook them for 45 minutes, until their internal temperature reaches 145°F.

7. Once they're cooked through, remove the ribs from the foil and place them directly on the grill grate. Using a basting brush, baste the ribs on all sides with the barbecue sauce.

8. Cook the brushed ribs for 10 more minutes, allowing the sauce to caramelize. Remove from the heat and serve immediately.

COOKING TIP: If you don't want to deal with potential leaking when wrapping your ribs in aluminum foil, you can use an aluminum pan with foil wrapped over the top instead. This is a way to make life easier—after all, there's not much worse than walking out to ripped foil, burnt ribs, and liquid evaporated and crusted onto your drain pan.

Twice-Baked Bangers and Mash

SERVES	PREP TIME	SMOKE TEMPERATURE
8	20 minutes	400°F, then 300°F
	SMOKE TIME	WOOD PELLET FLAVOR
	1 hour 5 minutes	Hickory

ORIGINALLY FROM THE United Kingdom, bangers and mash is one of Britain's best-known dishes. Consisting of sausage and mashed potatoes, it makes for a perfect festive meal, and it's an easy one at that. Traditional bangers and mash is plenty delicious, but we can take it to the next level with a pellet grill. To get that full, wood-fired flavor, we take bangers and "mash" them up with twice-baked potatoes for an all-American twist on the British original.

4 russet potatoes

8 sausages (Cumberland pork sausage is traditional, but your favorite will work in its place)

10 tablespoons butter

Salt

Freshly ground black pepper

2 teaspoons garlic powder

½ cup milk

1. Supply your smoker with wood pellets and follow the manufacturer's specific start-up procedure. Preheat the grill, with the lid closed, to 400°F.

2. Wash and scrub the potatoes, then prick them with a fork to create holes for steam to escape. Once the grill reaches 400°F, set the potatoes directly on the grill grate, and cook them until they're soft enough that they can easily be poked with a fork—usually around 45 minutes.

3. Reduce the grill temperature to 300°F and place the sausages on the grill. Remove the potatoes from the grill.

4. While the sausages are cooking, slice the potatoes in half lengthwise. Use a spoon to scoop out the insides of the potatoes, being careful not to tear the skins, and transfer the flesh to a large mixing bowl. Set the skins aside—you'll use them later.

5. Add the butter, salt, pepper, garlic powder, and milk to the bowl with the potato flesh. Mix until well incorporated.

6. Scoop the potato mixture back into the potato skins and carefully return them to the grill. Top each potato half with one of the sausages.

7. Cook the potatoes and sausages for 20 more minutes, or until both the potatoes and sausages are heated completely through. Remove them from the heat and serve immediately.

COOKING TIP: For additional flavor, top your Twice-Baked Bangers and Mash with sautéed caramelized onions and brown gravy. You can cook the onions in a cast-iron skillet right on the grill, making this an easy addition to the dish.

Classic Pork Chops

SERVES	PREP TIME	SMOKE TEMPERATURE
4	5 minutes	350°F
	SMOKE TIME	WOOD PELLET FLAVOR
	25 minutes	Maple

PORK CHOPS WILL always have a place at the classic American dinner table. Served with sides like mashed potatoes and green beans, I can't think of a dish that better exemplifies Americana. The great thing about pork chops is that they have their own awesome flavor. Pork chops are one of those meats that need next to no seasoning. For this cook, we're going to throw on just a little salt and pepper and let the flavors of the maple wood and meat shine.

Salt	Freshly ground black pepper	4½ pounds pork chops

1. Supply your smoker with wood pellets and follow the manufacturer's specific start-up procedure. Preheat the grill, with the lid closed, to 350°F.

2. Salt and pepper the pork chops all over, using your hands to rub the seasonings into the meat.

3. Once the grill reaches 350°F, place the pork chops directly on the grill. Cook them for about 25 minutes, until their internal temperature reaches 145°F.

4. Remove the pork chops from the grill and let them rest for 5 minutes before serving.

COOKING TIP: Mixed Veggies (page 115) and Grilled Brussels Sprouts (page 118) both make perfect sides for pork chops; their earthiness serves as a great complement to the saltiness of the pork.

BEGINNER'S BRISKET ★ 74

BEEF AND OTHER MEATS

MUCH OF our time spent at the barbecue revolves around beef. Between steaks, brisket, ribs, and roasts, beef has much to offer, and this chapter takes full advantage. A basic steak is always great, and might be what we cook most often, but in this chapter, I'll also make sure you are well versed in how to prepare several cuts of beef, including brisket, prime rib, and even tomahawks, on the wood pellet grill and smoker. In addition to the beef, we'll also get an introduction to lamb and bison to round out your red meat skill set.

BEEF CUTS

Most butcher cases have a wide range of beef cuts, and as you get more comfortable with your pellet grill, you'll discover your favorite options. I spend most of my time at the pellet grill cooking brisket, roasts, ribs, and steaks.

Steaks can range from the higher priced, like fatty rib eyes and tender filet mignon to the leaner, cheaper choices, like round steak and sirloin. My favorite steaks are New York strips. Roasts are another wide-ranging cut, with tri-tip, round roasts, and more. Brisket can be sold as a whole packer brisket or as a flat (for slicing) or point (for burnt ends). Ribs can be short and flat, enormous (see dino ribs), or ultra fatty, as in a rib roast.

The quality of a given cut of beef is typically labeled by grade, with "choice" and "prime" being what you find most frequently at the market. Prime is the more marbled, higher-quality grade. The other type of beef to look out for is wagyu. This heavily marbled beef is high priced and highly sought after. I have to say my best grilled steaks have been wagyu beef.

LAMB AND GAME GREATNESS

Lamb and game meats are both better when cooked on a pellet grill, and you'll get an introduction to both in this chapter. Lamb is often described as having a generic "gamey" flavor, but different cuts have different tastes, and your pellet grill can give you fantastic-tasting, rich results. At the grocery store, you'll typically find lamb in the form of leg of lamb, lamb chops, and ribs. In this chapter we will cover rib chops, my personal favorite cut of lamb.

Game meats can vary widely, but we'll get our feet wet by grilling up some easy bison burgers. Aside from bison, other popular game meats in North America include elk, venison, gator, and more. To learn more about cooking these meats, check out my other book, *Master the Wood Pellet Grill: A Cookbook to Smoke Meats and More Like a Pro.*

TECHNIQUES

Beef and other game can be prepared in many ways, from low and slow to a high-temperature sear. With beef, we're working to lock as many juices inside the meat as possible. Though convection-style cooking works well on its own, there are other things that we can do to supplement it. The first requires some patience and discipline: Let the meat rest after cooking. Trust that your meat is not complete until it has rested its suggested time. In this chapter, I'll give required rest times whenever necessary.

Check the temperature often. Especially when searing meat, even a few minutes can make a huge difference in internal temperature. A meat thermometer will take out the guesswork, ensuring you achieve the right level of doneness and don't run into any unwanted surprises.

Use foil or butcher paper to wrap your meats, especially for longer cooks involving smoking. Smoking can suck the moisture out of the meat, and wrapping the meat after smoking will help it retain as much moisture as possible as you continue to cook it.

With that said, don't be afraid to baste and spritz. You can bring moisture back into the meat by frequent spritzing or basting during grilling. Fruit juices, like apple juice, are great choices for this.

PRO TIPS

→ Some marbling is good, but you want to avoid overly fatty pieces of meat—I'm talking solid, thick pieces of fat. Brisket in particular can have huge fatty areas, and while some is good, if there's too much, you'll end up spending most of your time trimming the excess off before you even start grilling.

→ Know what internal temperature you're aiming for and check consistently. I'll start you off here: Internal temperatures for steak are 135°F for rare, 145°F for medium, and 155°F for well done.

→ Use beef broth to braise your meat when you wrap. This will add moisture that can get lost when smoking, and you won't take away from the meat's true flavor.

→ Do not—I repeat, *do not*—take brisket off the grill early; that is, unless you like the taste of leather. Brisket needs to be cooked to an internal temperature of at least 185°F, and for the most tender results it should really go higher. It can be tempting to cut corners, but I promise the low-and-slow method is worth it.

Reverse-Seared Tri-Tip

SERVES 4	PREP TIME 10 minutes	SMOKE TEMPERATURE 180°F, then 500°F
	SMOKE TIME 2 to 3 hours	WOOD PELLET FLAVOR Mesquite

MY FAVORITE CUT of any meat is tri-tip. I love the way it is cooked, its flavor, and its texture—it's safe to say I am on board with all things tri-tip. I tend to cook tri-tip once every few weeks, and I am always in love with how it turns out. Because pellet grills are so effective at holding in a given cut of meat's moisture, tri-tip will make for an awesome pellet-grilled meal pretty much no matter how you prep it. That said, we'll start out this chapter with my all-time favorite method for tri-tip: the reverse sear.

Salt	Freshly ground black pepper	1½ pound tri-tip roast

1. Supply your smoker with wood pellets and follow the manufacturer's specific start-up procedure. Preheat the grill, with the lid closed, to 180°F.

2. Salt and pepper the tri-tip, using your hands to rub in the seasoning all over.

3. Once the grill reaches 180°F, place the tri-tip directly on the grill grate. Smoke the tri-tip until its internal temperature reaches 135°F, 2 to 3 hours.

4. Now it's time to give the tri-tip a quick sear. Once the tri-tip reaches 135°F, crank the grill's temperature all the way up to 500°F. Continue cooking the tri-tip until its internal temperature reaches 145°F, around 10 minutes or so. If your grill has an open-flame option, I recommend using it here and flipping the meat every 1 to 2 minutes.

5. Once it's cooked through, remove the tri-tip roast and let it rest for 10 minutes before slicing and serving.

COOKING TIP: I highly recommend using tri-tip for your next French dip–style sandwiches. Toast sandwich buns on the grill while the meat is resting and portion the meat directly on the bread just after slicing. Top it off with 1 or 2 slices of Swiss cheese and serve with your favorite au jus!

Beginner's Brisket

SERVES	PREP TIME	SMOKE TEMPERATURE
8 to 12	15 minutes	225°F, then 350°F
	SMOKE TIME	WOOD PELLET FLAVOR
	14 to 16 hours	Hickory

BRISKET IS ONE of the most sought-after meats to prepare on the pellet grill, and it's often considered one of the most difficult, but it doesn't have to be. I've fielded countless concerns from owners cooking brisket: first, about temperature swings, and second, about the grill running out of pellets mid-cook. You know now that temperature swings are a normal part of the process during low-and-slow smokes. With regard to the pellets, well, this is simply a matter of checking the hopper throughout your longer-running cooks. I typically don't go over four hours without checking my grill and hopper, refilling as necessary. If you've made it this far, you know that cooking brisket on a pellet grill can be easy—as long as you're familiar with the pellet grill's ability to cook low and long, this one should be a breeze.

1 (12-pound) full packer brisket	2 tablespoons yellow mustard	2 batches Brisket Rub (page 153)

1. Supply your smoker with wood pellets and follow the manufacturer's specific start-up procedure. Preheat the grill, with the lid closed, to 225°F.

2. Using a stiff boning knife, carefully remove all but about ½ inch of the large layer of fat (the fat cap) that covers one side of the brisket.

3. Rub the brisket all over with the mustard, then season it with the brisket rub, using your hands to rub it into the meat.

4. Once the grill reaches 225°F, place the brisket on the grill grate, fat-side down. Smoke the brisket until its internal temperature reaches 160°F, for as long as 8 to 10 hours. By this point, the brisket should form a dark bark.

5. Pull the brisket from the grill and wrap it generously in either foil or butcher paper, then set aside. Increase the pellet-grill temperature to 350°F. This might be a good time to top up the grill's pellet supply.

6. Once the grill reaches to 350°F, return the wrapped brisket to the grill. Continue cooking the brisket until its internal temperature reaches 190°F, around another 6 hours.

7. Once the brisket's internal temperature reaches 190°F, pull it from the grill. Set it aside to rest for 1 to 2 hours.

8. Once it's rested, unwrap the brisket. Separate the brisket point (the thicker, fattier section) from the flat (the larger, leaner section). Slice the flat, working against the grain. You can save the brisket point to make barbecue burnt ends, or slice it and serve it as well.

COOKING TIP: If you don't want to wrap the brisket, you can also cook it unwrapped. If you do this, just continue smoking it at 225°F (instead of increasing the heat to 350°F) until its internal temperature reaches 190°F. This method typically requires spritzing the brisket with apple juice or some other liquid to ensure the meat doesn't dry out during cooking.

Holiday Prime Rib

SERVES	PREP TIME	SMOKE TEMPERATURE
4 to 6	15 minutes	400°F
	SMOKE TIME	WOOD PELLET FLAVOR
	4 hours	Oak

COOKING PRIME RIB is a tradition for many of us, especially around the holidays. All through December and January, prime rib with a helping of horseradish is seemingly ubiquitous at the company parties and holiday gatherings I go to. Our pellet grill gives us the ability to cook prime rib at a consistent high heat while still giving it that amazingly juicy center. For this reason, roasting your prime rib at high heat is optimal for the best results—the convection of the pellet grill will give you a juicy cut, but the high heat will work with the fat of the meat to create a perfect crust.

1 (3-bone) rib roast	Salt	Freshly ground black pepper

1. Supply your smoker with wood pellets and follow the manufacturer's specific start-up procedure. Preheat the grill, with the lid closed, to 400°F.

2. Season the rib roast with salt and pepper all over, using your hands to rub the seasonings into the meat.

3. Once the grill reaches 400°F, place the rib roast directly on the grill grate. Cook it for about 4 hours, until the internal temperature of the meat reaches 130°F for medium-rare.

4. Once cooked to your preference, remove the rib roast from the grill. Let it rest for 15 minutes before slicing and serving.

COOKING TIP: Even though I typically suggest serving meat with little in the way of bells and whistles, I actually do recommend serving prime rib with a helping of horseradish. The heat of the horseradish complements the meat perfectly—after all, there's a reason it's a holiday tradition.

Reverse-Seared Tomahawk

SERVES	PREP TIME	SMOKE TEMPERATURE
2 to 3	15 minutes	180°F, then 400°F
	SMOKE TIME	WOOD PELLET FLAVOR
	1 to 2 hours	Hickory

THERE'S NOT MUCH you can pull off the grill that's as showstopping as a tomahawk steak. These rib-eye steaks with the bone intact get their name from the tomahawk axe: The big old rib bone coming out the end represents the handle of the axe, and the huge slab of meat at the end represents the blade. Of course, once your guests actually take a bite of your pellet-smoked tomahawk, they'll be even more impressed. The reverse-searing technique used here will provide all sorts of smoky flavor while sealing in all the good juices with a nice sear at the end.

2 tablespoons olive oil

1 (3-pound) tomahawk steak (bone-in rib eye with long, intact rib bone)

1 batch Brisket Rub (page 153)

2 tablespoons butter

1. Supply your smoker with wood pellets and follow the manufacturer's specific start-up procedure. Preheat the grill, with the lid closed, to 180°F.

2. Rub the olive oil onto the tomahawk steak all over, then rub in the brisket rub.

3. Place the steak directly on the grill and smoke it until its internal temperature reaches 135°F, about 1 hour depending on size. Remove the steak from the grill, set it aside, and increase the grill temperature to 400°F.

4. Now you'll give the tomahawk a sear. Once the grill reaches 400°F, set a large cast-iron skillet in the center of the grill. Put the steak in the cast iron and add the butter, which will ensure the steak doesn't stick.

5. Cook the steak in the cast iron until its internal temperature reaches 145°F, flipping once so it sears on both sides (about 10 minutes per side). Use a spoon to baste the steak with butter throughout cooking to penetrate it with more flavor. Remove the steak from the skillet, slice it against the grain, and serve immediately.

Dry-Brined New York Strips

SERVES	PREP TIME	SMOKE TEMPERATURE
4	15 minutes, plus 1 hour dry brining	375°F
		WOOD PELLET FLAVOR
	SMOKE TIME 20 to 30 minutes	Oak

I SPEND MUCH of my social-media life on Instagram. I post plenty of my own cooks and help others with theirs, but I also spend a ton of time looking for ideas, too. Some of my favorite chefs and barbecuers are on Instagram, from the king of Louisiana outdoor cooking, Jay Ducote, to German barbecuer Sascha Lotzmann. I've come up with some of my greatest cooks by watching theirs. Dry brining is one of the skills I picked up from Instagram. I saw the amazing color that came from dry-brined meat, and I knew I had to try it. After mastering it, I can safely say that dry brining your steaks will create a red color that pops onscreen and a deeper flavor that pops on your tongue.

4 (1-inch-thick) New York strip steaks

Sea salt

Freshly ground black pepper

1. Season the steaks with salt and pepper on both sides. Transfer the steaks to a wire rack set over a baking sheet. Leave in the refrigerator to dry brine for at least 1 hour and up to 24 hours, if possible.

2. Supply your smoker with wood pellets and follow the manufacturer's specific start-up procedure. Preheat the grill, with the lid closed, to 375°F.

3. Place the dry-brined steaks on the grill and cook for 20 to 30 minutes, until their internal temperature reaches 145°F for medium-rare.

4. Remove the steaks from the grill and let rest for 5 minutes before serving.

COOKING TIP: Don't judge the internal temperature of all steaks by taking the temperature of just one. All grills have hot spots, and one guaranteed way to end up with over- or undercooked meat is by not checking the internal temperature of each individual cut. It takes only a minute to check your steaks' temperature, and it's well worth it to do so for best results.

Bethany Chili Chipper

SERVES	PREP TIME	SMOKE TEMPERATURE
3 to 5	10 minutes	400°F
	SMOKE TIME	WOOD PELLET FLAVOR
	25 minutes	Alder

FROM THE '90S through the 2000s, high school boys from Silverton and Mt. Angel, Oregon, were known to load into cars and pickup trucks and fly down the road (at a very safe speed, of course) to Bethany Market, in the small community of Bethany, a few miles outside the towns. There were a few food options at Bethany Market, and most revolved around chili, country gravy, and Fritos. The Chili Chipper was the most popular of all. Though the market has since closed, many of us with fond memories of the place still re-create the meal at home. My version, of course, comes with some pellet-grill flair.

1 (14-ounce) bag corn chips (such as Fritos)

1 (15-ounce) can chili

2 cups shredded cheddar cheese

¼ cup sliced jalapeños

1 cup shredded lettuce

½ cup Smoked Salsa (page 139)

1 (2.5-ounce) can sliced olives

¼ cup chopped white onion

¼ cup sour cream

1. Supply your smoker with wood pellets and follow the manufacturer's specific start-up procedure. Preheat the grill, with the lid closed, to 400°F.

2. Pour the corn chips into a cast-iron skillet, spreading them in an even layer. Cover the chips with a layer of chili, then the shredded cheddar cheese and the jalapeños.

3. Once the grill has reached 400°F, place the skillet in the center of the grill. Cook the mixture for about 25 minutes, until the chili is hot and the cheese has melted.

4. Remove the skillet from the grill and top the chili with the shredded lettuce, salsa, olives, onion, and sour cream. Serve immediately, portioning into bowls.

COOKING TIP: Chili Chipper can accommodate meat as well: Add leftover pulled pork, steak, brisket, or whatever you have available for a more protein-packed meal. If you do this, add 3 to 5 minutes to the cook time to ensure the chili is fully cooked and heated through.

Jackie's Steak Stroganoff

SERVES 4 to 6	PREP TIME 15 minutes	SMOKE TEMPERATURE 400°F
	SMOKE TIME 30 minutes	WOOD PELLET FLAVOR Alder

WHEN I WAS growing up, one of my favorite meals was beef stroganoff. My mom would cut up strips of beef and stand over the stove for hours, tending to the ingredients. When I left home and started cooking for myself, stroganoff was something I craved, but I never had the energy to spend my evening standing over a kitchen stove. It wasn't until a few years ago that I asked my mom for the recipe so I could make it into something of my own, all cooked on the pellet grill. Over time, my mom's original recipe began to morph as I adapted it for grilling. Here's my version as it exists today.

2 pounds round steak

Salt

Freshly ground
black pepper

4 tablespoons butter

1 cup chopped onion

2 tablespoons flour

1 (14.5-ounce) can
beef broth

1 tablespoon
Worcestershire sauce

2 teaspoons salt

2 tablespoons
tomato paste

1 cup sour cream

1 (16-ounce) box pasta
of your choice,
cooked to package
directions, for serving

1. Supply your smoker with wood pellets and follow the manufacturer's specific start-up procedure. Preheat the grill, with the lid closed, to 400°F.

2. Season the steaks on either side with salt and pepper.

3. Once the grill reaches 400°F, set a cast-iron skillet in the center of the grill to preheat it. Place the steaks directly on the grill grate, on either side of the skillet.

4. Cook the steaks until their internal temperature reaches 145°F, then pull the meat from the grill and thinly slice it against the grain. Set aside.

5. Melt the butter in the skillet. Once the butter is melted, add the onion and cook until soft, about 4 minutes.

6. Add the flour, beef broth, and Worcestershire sauce, and stir frequently, until the mixture thickens. Add the salt, tomato paste, and sour cream, and stir to incorporate.

7. Add the sliced steak back into the skillet and stir to incorporate, ensuring everything is well mixed. Remove the skillet from the grill and serve hot with your favorite noodles (my personal favorite is rotini).

COOKING TIP: You can use any type of steak for this dish, depending on what you can get. Any steak, including the other cuts mentioned in this book (like sirloin, top round, and tri-tip), are all great for beef stroganoff.

Seared Lamb Chops

SERVES	PREP TIME	SMOKE TEMPERATURE
4	10 minutes	500°F
	SMOKE TIME	WOOD PELLET FLAVOR
	15 minutes	Maple

LAMB CHOPS ARE an awesome, underrated meat that in my opinion many of us don't get to try often enough. A good lamb chop is not something that you can find at your average local restaurant, but your pellet grill can cook up some amazing ones in a jiff. There are a few types of lamb chops to choose from; the flavorful shoulder chops and lean loin chops tend to be the most popular. For this recipe, I use the tender rib chops and serve them with a mint jelly.

4½ pounds bone-in lamb chops

2 tablespoons olive oil

Salt

Freshly ground black pepper

Mint jelly, for serving

1. Supply your smoker with wood pellets and follow the manufacturer's specific start-up procedure. Preheat the grill, with the lid closed, to 500°F.

2. Rub the lamb chops with oil all over, then season them with salt and pepper.

3. Once the grill reaches 500°F, place the lamb chops directly on the grill grate. Cook them to your preference—their internal temperature should reach 120°F for rare, 130°F for medium, and 145°F for well (between 10 and 20 minutes, depending).

4. Once they're ready, remove the chops from the grill and serve them immediately, with the mint jelly.

COOKING TIP: Lamb also goes very well with rosemary. When seasoning the lamb chops, try sprinkling them with 1½ teaspoons of dry rosemary, or use a store-bought rosemary-based rub.

Beef Jerky

SERVES	PREP TIME	SMOKE TEMPERATURE
6 to 8	25 minutes, plus overnight marinating	180°F
	SMOKE TIME	WOOD PELLET FLAVOR
	4 to 5 hours	Hickory

SO MANY BARBECUE fans love beef jerky, and the market prices it accordingly! I can't tell you the number of times that I've dropped $10 on a bag of jerky only to finish it by myself in one sitting. One of the best parts of owning a smoker is that you no longer have to pay sky-high prices for good jerky—you can do it all at home for a fraction of the cost. Your pellet grill works great to smoke beef efficiently and with fantastic flavor, since it can maintain consistent low temperatures for a long time in order to imbue the meat with plenty of smoky flavor.

1 pound top round roast

Beef Marinade
  (page 147)

Salt

Freshly ground
  black pepper

1. Slice the top round roast into ½-inch-thick pieces, cutting against the grain of the meat. Put the sliced beef into a gallon-size resealable plastic bag. Pour in the marinade and leave in the refrigerator to marinate overnight.

2. The next day, supply your smoker with wood pellets and follow the manufacturer's specific start-up procedure. Preheat the grill, with the lid closed, to 180°F.

3. Remove the sliced roast from the marinade and season it all over with salt and pepper. Place the sliced meat directly on the grill grate to smoke, using multiple racks if necessary.

4. Allow the meat to smoke for 4 to 5 hours, until the jerky is dry but still bendable. Remove the jerky from the heat and serve or store in an airtight container at room temperature.

COOKING TIP: I use top round roast most frequently for jerky, but I do so because it's usually the most affordable cut I can find. If you have a roast that you prefer or can acquire for a better price, feel free to switch the cut and do the rest of the recipe the same way.

Beef Short Ribs

SERVES	PREP TIME	SMOKE TEMPERATURE
2 to 4	5 minutes	225°F
	SMOKE TIME	WOOD PELLET FLAVOR
	5 to 7 hours	Mesquite

EARLY ON IN my cooking experience, I thought short ribs had to be prepped the same way as any other ribs—and while they definitely can be cooked that way, there's so much more to get out of them through braising and smoking. For this cook, we're going to do a long smoke, which is going to give us ultra-flavorful, super-tender, fall-off-the-bone ribs. Beef short ribs are fatty enough that this longer cook won't dry them out, but if you're worried, you can always spritz them with apple juice for some additional moisture, flavor, and peace of mind.

4 beef short ribs

1 batch Brisket Rub
(page 153)

1. Supply your smoker with wood pellets and follow the manufacturer's specific start-up procedure. Preheat the grill, with the lid closed, to 225°F.

2. Season the short ribs all over with the brisket rub, rubbing it thoroughly into the meat.

3. Once the grill reaches 225°F, add the ribs to the grill. Allow them to smoke for 5 to 7 hours—their internal temperature should reach 200°F.

4. Pull the ribs from the grill and let them rest for 30 minutes before serving.

COOKING TIP: Short ribs are good practice for making brisket. The smoke, texture, and flavor of short ribs is fairly similar to brisket, but short ribs are a shorter cook, allowing you to watch your grill and understand how it works and how the beef reacts to temperature.

Bison Burgers

SERVES	PREP TIME	SMOKE TEMPERATURE
4	15 minutes	400°F
	SMOKE TIME	WOOD PELLET FLAVOR
	25 minutes	Competition Blend

BISON HAS MADE quite a name for itself on the market in recent years. As a leaner but just-as-delicious alternative to beef, there's no question why. Bison is available in far more forms nowadays than in previous years, and ground bison is relatively easy to find at your local supermarket (it'll most commonly be in the frozen section). Pick up a package, let it defrost, and get ready to grill up some quick burgers after work.

1 pound ground bison

1 large egg

1 batch Brisket Rub (page 153)

4 hamburger buns

Toppings of your choice, for serving

1. Supply your smoker with wood pellets and follow the manufacturer's specific start-up procedure. Preheat the grill, with the lid closed, to 400°F.

2. In a large mixing bowl, combine the ground bison and the egg. Use (clean) hands to mix them together until well combined.

3. Divide the bison and egg mixture into 4 equal portions and form into patties. Season the patties on both sides with the brisket rub.

4. Once the grill reaches 400°F, place the bison burgers directly on the grill and cook until their internal temperature reaches 145°, about 25 minutes.

5. Remove the burgers from the grill, set them on the buns, and add toppings of your choosing. Serve immediately.

COOKING TIP: Since bison's popularity is often due to it being a healthier alternative to beef, you could embrace the health-conscious vibe and wrap these burgers in lettuce leaves instead of buns.

Street Tacos

SERVES	PREP TIME	SMOKE TEMPERATURE
4 to 5	15 minutes	500°F
	SMOKE TIME	WOOD PELLET FLAVOR
	20 minutes	Hickory

TACOS ARE ANOTHER already-fantastic food made even better with the help of a pellet grill. By using wood-fired steaks as your meat, rather than ground beef or other stove-cooked options, you can give your tacos a smoky flavor that'll give even the best street tacos a run for their money. I like to use a sirloin steak for my tacos, since I have the perfect amount of time to prep the rest of the taco ingredients while the meat cooks on the grill, making for a quick meal that's dressed to impress.

FOR THE STEAK

2 pounds sirloin steak

Salt

Freshly ground
    black pepper

FOR THE TACOS

½ white onion

1 bunch cilantro

2 limes

10 (5-inch) flour or
    corn tortillas

TO MAKE THE STEAK

1. Supply your smoker with wood pellets and follow the manufacturer's specific start-up procedure. Preheat the grill, with the lid closed, to 500°F.

2. Season the steaks with salt and pepper on both sides.

3. Once the grill reaches 500°F, place the steaks on the grill grate and cook until their internal temperature reaches 145°F, about 20 minutes. This is a good time to prep the rest of the taco ingredients.

4. Once they're cooked, remove the steaks from the grill and let them rest for 5 minutes before slicing them into thin strips.

5. While the steaks are cooking, prepare the other ingredients for the tacos: Finely dice the onion, chop the cilantro leaves (discard the stems), and cut the limes into quarters.

6. Evenly divide the sliced steak among the tortillas and garnish with the onion and cilantro. Squeeze lime juice over them and serve immediately.

COOKING TIP: Rather than using salt and pepper, you can try using taco seasoning or another chile-based rub to season your steaks, adding a little bit of heat.

Bold Beef Kebabs

SERVES	PREP TIME	SMOKE TEMPERATURE
4 to 6	25 minutes	400°F

	SMOKE TIME	WOOD PELLET FLAVOR
	15 minutes	Mesquite

KEBABS ARE A go-to in the barbecue world, and a crowd pleaser to boot. The reasons are obvious: They're loaded with meat, they give you the option to load up on vegetables (and sometimes fruit, like pineapple), and they're a blast to serve. Beef kebabs are my favorite by a long shot. The beef flavor is perfectly complemented with onions, tomatoes, and bell peppers. This is a simple dish that's as fun to make as it is to eat.

½ white onion

1 green bell pepper

1 red bell pepper

½ pound cherry tomatoes

2 pounds sirloin steak, cut into 1-inch cubes

Salt

Freshly ground black pepper

1. Cut the onion and bell peppers into 1-inch chunks (but leave the cherry tomatoes whole).

2. Supply your smoker with wood pellets and follow the manufacturer's specific start-up procedure. Preheat the grill, with the lid closed, to 400°F.

3. Meanwhile, thread the meat and vegetables onto wood skewers, alternating between meat and vegetables. Leave a small gap between the pieces to avoid crowding, and allow for about 2 to 3 empty inches on each end of the skewers.

4. Season the kebabs with salt and pepper. Once the grill reaches 400°F, place the kebabs directly on the grill and cook until the internal temperature of the meat reaches at least 140°F—about 15 minutes.

5. Once they're cooked to your preference, remove the kebabs from the grill and serve immediately, on the skewers if desired.

COOKING TIP: When using wood skewers, make sure you soak them in water for 30 to 60 minutes before using them on the grill. Using dry skewers can cause the wood to burn, leaving you with brittle black stubs to hold.

FISH AND SEAFOOD

GROWING UP in a coastal state, I've been lucky to spend my entire life enjoying quality seafood. Even better, I have enjoyed it straight off the pellet grill. While salmon is the most commonly found fish in the Pacific Northwest, there are many seafood selections available to us here. I encourage you to visit your local seafood market and check out what looks good to you.

|||||||| FROM THE SEA TO THE SMOKER ||||||||

When grilling with seafood, we have a variety of options available. Unlike meats, which are different cuts of the same few animals, with seafood we are often dealing with completely different species. Fish, crustaceans, and mollusks are all seafood, but they're all distinctly different and offer us a wide variety of flavor profiles and textures.

Fish fall into two categories: seafood with flaky white flesh, like halibut and cod, and fish with pinker-toned flesh, like salmon and tuna. When it comes to crustaceans, such as shrimp, crawfish, and crab, we frequently cook them in the shell and pull out the cooked meat—though that is not always the case. With lobster, for instance, we often split the shell to expose the meat during cooking. Personally, with shrimp, I think pre-peeling is the way to go (see Cast-Iron Shrimp, page 99). With regard to mollusks, oysters, clams, and mussels are all commonly found around the barbecue. Mollusks can be cooked whole in their shells, making for a quick, clean, and low-maintenance cook.

|||||||||||||||||||||||||||| TECHNIQUES ||||||||||||||||||||||||||||

There are practically as many tips and tricks to cooking fish and seafood as there are types of fish in the sea. There are a few easy ones that will save you a lot of trouble. When cooking fish, salmon especially, you risk the skin sticking to the grill grates. This is annoying, and it can also cause the fish to fall apart as you pull it from the grill. To prevent this, coat your grill grates with vegetable or canola oil before you set the fish on the grill. Or set the fish on a soaked cedar plank while grilling. Cedar planks are available at many grocery stores and butcher shops; soak the plank overnight for the day you plan to grill.

When cooking fish, I also tend to stay low in temperature. Fish can be grilled hot—and we will do a bit of searing in this chapter (Simple Seared Tuna Steaks, page 96)—but most often I go low. This is to prevent the flesh from drying out, ensuring your finished product will be tender, moist, and flaky.

➡ Always use an instant-read thermometer when cooking fish. It's all too easy to overcook fish, drying it out. Luckily, it's also easy to prevent overcooking altogether by pulling fish off the grill right when it reaches the correct internal temperature, which for most fish is 145°F.

➡ If you like oysters, invest in a good oyster knife and some gloves. As someone who has used butter knives on oysters one too many times, I can tell you that having the right tools will make all the difference.

➡ Seafood likes citrus, and citrus likes seafood. I always like to serve seafood with a wedge of lemon on the side, but you should also use citrus-based spices on it before cooking, like the Lemon-Pepper Seafood Rub (page 155).

➡ Butter also complements most seafood well. You can use butter to dip your oysters in or to baste your smoked salmon. Adding butter to your seafood will give it tons of moisture and flavor.

Glazed Salmon

SERVES	PREP TIME	SMOKE TEMPERATURE
4	10 minutes	325°F
	SMOKE TIME	WOOD PELLET FLAVOR
	25 minutes	Alder

BECAUSE SALMON IS the predominant seafood here in the Pacific Northwest, it's no surprise that I've cooked salmon more than any other fish. Like most other fish, salmon can dry out during cooking if not properly attended. For this recipe, we'll use a balsamic glaze to combat dryness. Though the glaze works wonders to trap moisture, the most important thing to do is pull the fish off the grill right when its internal temperature hits 145°F. The longer the salmon stays on the grill, the drier it'll get, so pulling right at temp is your one-way ticket to perfect fish.

---

1 (2-pound) half salmon fillet

1 batch Lemon-Pepper Seafood Rub (page 155)

2 tablespoons balsamic glaze

1. Supply your smoker with wood pellets and follow the manufacturer's specific start-up procedure. Preheat the grill, with the lid closed, to 325°F.

2. Sprinkle the salmon fillet with the seafood rub. Once the grill reaches 325°F, place the salmon directly on the grill grate, skin-side down, and cook for about 20 minutes, or until its internal temperature just reaches 140°F—a few minutes from being cooked through.

3. Using a basting brush, coat the salmon with the balsamic glaze, completely covering the flesh of the fish. Continue cooking the salmon for a few more minutes, until its internal temperature reaches 145°F. Remove the salmon from the grill and serve immediately.

COOKING TIP: Use a salmon spatula or an oversize metal grilling spatula when taking the salmon off the grill. A large spatula will prevent the fish from breaking.

Cajun Crab Cakes

SERVES	PREP TIME	SMOKE TEMPERATURE
4	15 minutes, plus 1 hour resting	350°F
		WOOD PELLET FLAVOR
	SMOKE TIME	Competition Blend
	20 minutes	

CRAB CAKES PACK a ton of awesome flavor in a small package. They're usually fried or baked, and to a beginner they can seem intimidating to make. But in reality, crab cakes are a great and easy fit for a pellet grill. For this cook, we'll be using the baking technique adapted for the pellet grill to add woodiness, giving these already-rich cakes even more depth of flavor. The crab cake mixture gets better with time, so I recommend mixing the ingredients together a day ahead (or the morning of) so they have maximum flavor once they hit the grill.

½ cup mayonnaise

1 large egg

2 teaspoons Dijon mustard

1 tablespoon Worcestershire sauce

2 teaspoons Blackened Cajun Rub (page 152)

1 pound crab meat

½ cup crushed butter crackers (about 15 crackers; I use Ritz)

1. Supply your smoker with wood pellets and follow the manufacturer's specific start-up procedure. Preheat the grill, with the lid closed, to 350°F.

2. In a medium mixing bowl, combine the mayonnaise, egg, mustard, Worcestershire sauce, rub, and crab meat. Stir to incorporate. Add the crushed crackers and stir to incorporate. Cover the bowl and refrigerate for at least 1 hour, or up to 24 hours, before forming the crab cakes.

3. Once it's rested, use your hands to form the crab cake mixture into eight equal-size patties. Place the patties directly on the grill grate. Cook the crab cakes until golden brown, roughly 20 minutes, flipping halfway through.

COOKING TIP: Using salmon instead of crab gives a different flavor to this old-school favorite. As a kid, one of my favorite foods was the salmon cakes my parents made on their pellet grill. You can easily swap the same amount of chopped-up salmon meat for the crab meat in this preparation.

Simple Seared Tuna Steaks

SERVES	PREP TIME	SMOKE TEMPERATURE
2	5 minutes	500°F
	SMOKE TIME	WOOD PELLET FLAVOR
	5 minutes	Hickory

TUNA STEAKS ARE a simple but hearty and flavorful cut of fish. Tuna steaks are often available "sushi grade," meaning they can be eaten raw. Sushi grade is the highest grade given to fish, so if you see it, you'll know that the quality and the flavor are there. To work with this flavorful fish, we won't do much to the meat: It's lightly seasoned and cooked hot and very fast to create a crispy seared outside with a raw, tender inside.

1 batch Lemon-Pepper
   Seafood Rub
   (page 155)

2 sushi-grade tuna
   steaks, sliced
   2 inches thick

1. Supply your smoker with wood pellets and follow the manufacturer's specific start-up procedure. Preheat the grill, with the lid closed, to 500°F.

2. Rub the seafood rub into the tuna steaks, covering them completely. (If you want to keep it even simpler, you can simply use salt and freshly ground black pepper instead.)

3. Place the tuna steaks directly on the grill grate. Sear the steaks for 2 to 3 minutes on one side, then flip and sear for 2 to 3 more minutes. Once their internal temperature has reached 115°F, remove the seared steaks and serve immediately.

COOKING TIP: Tuna steaks are the perfect fancy dish for date night! Pair the tuna with a side of Mixed Veggies (page 115) and a light red wine. Not only will you get by with an easy, better-than-restaurant meal at a fraction of the cost, you can also use the time you saved on dinner prep to clean yourself up for that special someone.

Grilled-Scallop Skewers

SERVES	PREP TIME	SMOKE TEMPERATURE
4	10 minutes	375°F
	SMOKE TIME	WOOD PELLET FLAVOR
	10 minutes	Mesquite

GRILLED SCALLOPS ARE amazing and quick to cook, but they can be a little finicky in comparison with other types of seafood. The tender meat of the scallop tends to want to fall apart, making those perfect round scallops not so perfect when scraped off the grill. To combat this, we'll cook the scallops on skewers, which make them easier to prep, grill, and serve. Best of all, we'll serve these directly on the skewers—just make sure that if the kids are around, they don't use them to start a sword fight.

1 pound large scallops

2 tablespoons olive oil

1 batch Lemon-Pepper Seafood Rub (page 155)

1. Supply your smoker with wood pellets and follow the manufacturer's specific start-up procedure. Preheat the grill, with the lid closed, to 375°F.

2. Thread 4 to 5 scallops vertically onto each of four metal grill skewers, leaving a small space between each one. Once they're skewered, drizzle the scallops with the olive oil and sprinkle with the seafood rub.

3. Once the grill reaches 375°F, place the skewers directly on the grill grate. Grill the scallops for 5 minutes, then flip and grill on the other side for 5 more minutes. Remove the scallops from the grill and serve immediately.

COOKING TIP: Scallops are perfect on their own as a main or as a side. Try making these Grilled-Scallop Skewers for your next party, served alongside some Reverse-Seared Tri-Tip (page 73) for a festive surf 'n' turf barbecue.

Barbecued Halibut

SERVES 4	PREP TIME 5 minutes	SMOKE TEMPERATURE 275°F
	SMOKE TIME 35 minutes	WOOD PELLET FLAVOR Hickory

HALIBUT IS A mild-flavored and light-textured fish that lends itself well to taking on other flavors. For that reason, you may be most familiar with halibut served in the form of fish and chips. Though I am a huge fan of fish and chips, I think that one of the best and easiest ways to take advantage of halibut's mildness is to throw it on a pellet grill. That's what we'll do here, using a low-but-not-too-low temperature of 275°F. This temp will cook the halibut relatively quickly while also giving us some smoky flavor.

1 pound halibut fillet

1 batch Lemon-Pepper Seafood Rub (page 155)

Canola oil or cooking spray, for greasing the grill

1. Supply your smoker with wood pellets and follow the manufacturer's specific start-up procedure. Preheat the grill, with the lid closed, to 275°F.

2. Sprinkle the halibut fillet on both sides with the seafood rub.

3. Once the grill reaches a temperature of to 275°F, coat the grill grate with canola oil to prevent the fish from sticking to the grates.

4. Place the halibut on the grill grate and grill until its internal temperature reaches 145°F, about 35 minutes. Once cooked through, remove the halibut from the grill and serve immediately.

COOKING TIP: You may know by now that I always recommend making your own seasonings. With that said, I do have a few store-bought favorites. Other than the one I make, my favorite rub for seafood is Dilly-O Finishing Salt, made by an Oregon company called Salinity (after all, I love to shop local). Dilly-O salt has an awesome dill-and-onion flavor that goes amazingly well with seafood.

Cast-Iron Shrimp

SERVES	PREP TIME	SMOKE TEMPERATURE
4	10 minutes, plus 1 hour resting	400°F
		WOOD PELLET FLAVOR Alder
	SMOKE TIME 20 minutes	

THIS FOUR-INGREDIENT CAST-IRON braised shrimp is the most popular dish I cook on the grill. I seem to find a reason to cook it about once a week, and there are never any leftovers. If you haven't already, invest in a cast-iron skillet, not only for this recipe but for countless other pellet-grilling applications. My favorite cast iron is made by Petromax: a 12-inch skillet with two short handles that make it super easy to use directly on the grill.

1 pound shrimp with tails, peeled and deveined

1 batch Blackened Cajun Rub (page 152)

½ cup (1 stick) butter

¼ cup Worcestershire sauce

1. Coat the shrimp with the Cajun rub. Set aside in the refrigerator for at least 1 hour (or up to 12 hours) prior to grilling.

2. Supply your smoker with wood pellets and follow the manufacturer's specific start-up procedure. Set a cast-iron skillet on the grill and preheat, with the lid closed, to 400°F.

3. Once your grill has reached 400°F, put the stick of butter in the cast-iron skillet directly on the grill and allow it to melt. Once the butter is melted, stir in the Worcestershire sauce.

4. Add the seasoned shrimp to the skillet and braise them for about 10 minutes, then flip them and braise for 10 more minutes on the other side. Once cooked, the shrimp should be opaque. Remove them from the grill and serve immediately, drizzling with any extra juices from the cast iron.

COOKING TIP: There are plenty of varieties of shrimp preparations available at the grocery store, including lots of precooked versions that may be tempting. But before you choose something precooked, you should know that I've always had the best luck with the raw, peeled and deveined shrimp. Cooking the shrimp from raw allows the flavor to be fully cooked into it, and having it peeled before cooking ensures the flavoring doesn't end up peeling off with the shell.

Jambalaya

SERVES	PREP TIME	SMOKE TEMPERATURE
6	40 minutes	400°F
	SMOKE TIME	WOOD PELLET FLAVOR
	55 minutes	Alder

JAMBALAYA HAS BEEN my favorite food for some time, and I can't tell you the number of times I've seen jambalaya on a restaurant's menu and jumped to order it before I even read anything else. Being who I am, I had to try it on a pellet grill to get that smoky flavor. When I first tried to make my own jambalaya, I realized there weren't really any recipes that catered to a grill, let alone a pellet grill. Through looking at a few other jambalaya recipes and using my own recipes for chicken and shrimp, I created my own version. This isn't the easiest or fastest recipe in this book, but if you can put in the time, it's definitely one of the most fulfilling.

½ pound chicken tenders

1 batch Blackened Cajun Rub, divided (page 152)

½ batch Cast-Iron Shrimp (page 99)

½ pound andouille sausage

1 white onion

1 green bell pepper

1 red bell pepper

2 garlic cloves

1 tablespoon olive oil

1 (14.5-ounce) can chicken broth

14.5 ounces water

2 tablespoons tomato paste

1 cup long-grain rice

1. Supply your smoker with wood pellets and follow the manufacturer's specific start-up procedure. Set a cast-iron skillet on the grill and preheat, with the lid closed, to 400°F.

2. Rub the chicken tenders with half the Cajun rub. If you have not prepared the cast-iron shrimp, this would be a good time to get it on the grill.

3. Once you have the shrimp cooking, place the seasoned chicken tenders on the grill grate and cook until the internal temperature reaches 170°F, 15 to 20 minutes, flipping halfway through.

4. While the chicken is cooking, you can also add the sausage to the grill. Cook for about 10 minutes, or until the internal temperature reaches 145°F, turning halfway through.

5. Meanwhile, chop the onion and green and red bell peppers into ½-inch strips and mince the garlic. Set aside.

6. Remove the shrimp, chicken tenders, and andouille sausage from the grill. Slice the sausage and chicken into bite-size pieces. Transfer the shrimp to a separate bowl and set aside.

7. Return the skillet to the grill. Pour the olive oil into it and add the onion. Cook for 5 minutes, until slightly translucent, then add the bell peppers and garlic and cook for 5 more minutes, stirring occasionally, until the vegetables are slightly soft.

8. Add the chicken broth, water, tomato paste, and the remainder of the Cajun rub to the skillet, mixing completely. Stir in the rice, then add the chicken, andouille sausage, and shrimp. Toss to incorporate.

9. Continue cooking the jambalaya, stirring occasionally, until all the liquid is absorbed and the rice is soft, about 25 minutes. Remove the jambalaya from the grill and serve. Keep leftovers refrigerated for up to 4 days.

COOKING TIP: Use leftover meat and other protein to build the base for your jambalaya. When I cook a full chicken, I often tear the leftover meat off the bones and do jambalaya the next night—it's almost like getting two meals in one.

Smoked-Salmon Dip

SERVES	PREP TIME	SMOKE TEMPERATURE
10 to 12	15 minutes	180°F
	SMOKE TIME	WOOD PELLET FLAVOR
	4 to 5 hours	Mesquite

SMOKED SALMON IS something I just can't get enough of. A few years back, my friend Dennis was working in salmon fishing in Alaska. When he came back, he inundated me with salmon fillets. One of the things that came from this was a massive amount of salmon dip. We spent that entire summer smoking our own salmon and making a dip with whatever we didn't finish right away. This recipe is based on the dip we invented that summer, and it's been a hit at parties ever since.

FOR THE SMOKED SALMON

1 (1 pound) salmon fillet

1 batch Lemon-Pepper Seafood Rub (page 155)

FOR THE DIP

1 cup cream cheese

¼ cup mayonnaise

¼ cup sour cream

1 tablespoon freshly squeezed lemon juice

1 teaspoon hot sauce (such as Tapatío or Tabasco)

2 tablespoons dillweed

TO MAKE THE SMOKED SALMON

1. Supply your smoker with wood pellets and follow the manufacturer's specific start-up procedure. Preheat the grill, with the lid closed, to 180°F.

2. Sprinkle the salmon fillet with the seafood rub. Once the grill reaches 180°F, place the salmon on the grill grate, skin-side down, and smoke it for 4 to 5 hours.

3. Once the salmon's internal temperature reaches 145°F, remove the salmon from the grill and set aside to cool while you get everything ready for the dip.

TO MAKE THE DIP

4. In the last hour that the salmon is smoking, set out the cream cheese to soften to room temperature.

5. While the salmon is cooling, in a medium mixing bowl, combine the cream cheese, mayonnaise, sour cream, lemon juice, hot sauce, and dillweed. Stir together and set aside while the salmon finishes cooking.

6. Once the salmon is cool, transfer it to a cutting board. Peel the skin off the fillet and remove any pin bones. Roughly chop the salmon into pieces and add it to the bowl of dip.

7. Mix all the ingredients, including the salmon, together well. You can technically eat this dip right away, but for best results, refrigerate overnight to ensure the salmon's smoky flavor carries over to the dip. Refrigerate leftovers for up to one week.

COOKING TIP: I like to serve this dip with crackers, like Wheat Thins or Triscuits, but it would also be great spread on a toasted bagel for breakfast.

Grilled Oysters

SERVES	PREP TIME	SMOKE TEMPERATURE
4	10 minutes	375°F
	SMOKE TIME	WOOD PELLET FLAVOR
	10 minutes	Hickory

OYSTERS WERE PRACTICALLY made for the grill. They cook quickly and thoroughly, and, of course, they also gain that wood-fired taste that you won't get anywhere else. They also come in their own nature-packaged grill-safe shells. We enjoyed oysters regularly at my family's house growing up, and I love to make them for my own family today.

10 oysters in shells

1 batch Lemon-Pepper Seafood Rub (page 155)

1 lemon, quartered

1. Supply your smoker with wood pellets and follow the manufacturer's specific start-up procedure. Preheat the grill, with the lid closed, to 375°F.

2. Using an oyster knife, carefully remove the top shells of the oysters. As you do this, work gently, making sure to lose as little as possible of the juice inside the shells.

3. Sprinkle the oysters with the seafood rub. Once the grill reaches 375°F, place the oysters in their half shells directly on the grill grate.

4. Grill the oysters for 7 to 10 minutes, until fully cooked through (I find around 7 minutes is usually good). Remove the oysters from the grill, squeeze lemon juice over each one, and serve immediately.

COOKING TIP: I'm a huge fan of spicy foods, and oysters are no exception. When you add the lemon juice to your oysters, give them a splash of your favorite hot sauce to spice things up.

VEGETABLES AND SIDES

SOME OF the best creations that will come off your pellet grill and smoker will be veggies and other side dishes. The wood-fired flavor will help you make the best sides you've ever had, and the functionality and versatility of the pellet grill is perfectly suited for cooking them a few at a time or alongside main dishes.

GOING GREEN ON THE GRILL

So many of us are used to eating fruits and veggies prepared in an oven or on the stove top, but adding wood-fired flavor makes them so much better. The grill will give you texture and flavor results that are not possible indoors. While there are some fruits and vegetables that are obvious choices for the pellet grill, like Classic Potato Wedges (page 110) and Pellet-Grilled Corn on the Cob (page 116), there are some definite dark horses that you wouldn't think of, like Grilled Pineapple Slices (page 117) and Grilled Peaches (page 112).

The versatility of your pellet grill allows you to give all these different foods amazing, smoky flavor. Not every grill can adapt to cook these totally different types of food while not compromising on flavor or texture. Slow smoking, roasting, grilling, and other forms of pellet-grill cooking are all used in this chapter to round out your grilling game.

SIDE HUSTLE

With your pellet grill, you can cook outdoors every side that you would normally do indoors—and I'm talking real-deal sides, like Barbecued Nachos (page 120), Smoked Mac and Cheese (page 121), and Cheesy Tailgate Potatoes (page 119). Pellet grilling your sides allows you to keep the heat (and the mess) out of the kitchen and lets you do all your cooking in one place. Once you realize you can cook an entire meal on the grill, you won't look back. Very often, I time my meats and sides so I can finish them both on the grill at the same time and serve dinner in one fell swoop.

PRO TIPS

→ When cooking vegetables and other sides, cast iron is your best friend. It can absorb the heat of your grill, hold it, and distribute it evenly better than another pan would. It works wonders on many of these dishes.

→ Invest in either a veggie tray or basket, sometimes called a grill basket: It's a metal basket with small holes in it to place directly on your grill. Veggies are often cut too small to grill straight on the grate, so veggie baskets and trays keep them from falling through while ensuring enough airflow gets to them.

→ Make sure to pay attention to the consistency and firmness of the food you are cooking—on the grill, fruits and vegetables are not as forgiving as meat. If you cook them too long (or not long enough), your food could come off the grill undercooked, mushy, burnt, or utterly inedible. Veggies are easy with practice; you just might have to check on them more often when you start out.

→ A good set of griddle tools is a great addition to use with your grill and with cast iron. These steel tools, most importantly steel griddle spatulas, work great with the heat used to cook fruit and veggie sides—far better than a regular kitchen spatula.

Classic Potato Wedges

SERVES	PREP TIME	SMOKE TEMPERATURE
4 to 6	15 minutes	375°F
	SMOKE TIME	WOOD PELLET FLAVOR
	45 minutes	Oak

LIKE MANY OF the things that I cook most often, potato wedges are something I enjoyed growing up. Living in the home of some of the earliest adopters of the pellet grill, I learned early some of the best and most innovative ways to use the grill. Potato wedges were one of the sides we had most often, and nowadays I cook them for my own family. Potato wedges are especially popular with my kiddos, and in a house where other kinds of potatoes aren't usually a preferred choice, these wedges get eaten up quickly.

5 russet potatoes

3 tablespoons olive oil

Salt

Freshly ground black pepper

Ranch dip or dressing, for serving

1. Supply your smoker with wood pellets and follow the manufacturer's specific start-up procedure. Preheat the grill, with the lid closed, to 375°F.

2. Cut the potatoes lengthwise into eight wedges. Transfer them to a large mixing bowl and drizzle them with olive oil. Add salt and pepper to taste, and toss them to coat.

3. Once the grill reaches 375°F, transfer the potato wedges to the grill, skin-side down. Cook until they are fork-tender, around 45 minutes. Remove and serve with ranch dip on the side.

COOKING TIP: Malt vinegar and Slightly Spicy Barbecue Sauce (page 145) are also both great for dipping the potato wedges.

Bacon-Wrapped Asparagus

SERVES	PREP TIME	SMOKE TEMPERATURE
5 to 6	15 minutes	325°F

	SMOKE TIME	WOOD PELLET FLAVOR
	10 minutes	Hickory

I'M NOT GOING to lie: I'm not normally the biggest fan of asparagus. Its texture and flavor just don't do it for me, but my wife loves it. I also know that I'm in the minority with my distaste for it, so I end up making it relatively regularly. When guests visit, my wife often requests that I make asparagus, and I'm happy to cook up a helping with this crowd-pleasing technique using something that can put a vegetable over the top: bacon. Wrapping the asparagus in bacon will give it a salty, smoky flavor that is bound to impress a crowd.

12 asparagus spears

1 tablespoon olive oil

Salt

Freshly ground black pepper

6 slices bacon, sliced in half lengthwise

1. Supply your smoker with wood pellets and follow the manufacturer's specific start-up procedure. Preheat the grill, with the lid closed, to 325°F.

2. Coat the asparagus with the olive oil and season with salt and pepper. Wrap each spear of asparagus in a half slice of bacon, wrapping the bacon around the spear in a spiral.

3. Once the grill reaches 325°F, place the wrapped asparagus directly on the grill grate. Grill until the bacon is fully cooked, about 10 minutes. Remove from the grill and serve immediately.

COOKING TIP: When working with bacon, don't cook anything at too high a temperature. Temperatures of 400°F or higher can cause the bacon to cook too quickly and burn.

Grilled Peaches

SERVES	PREP TIME	SMOKE TEMPERATURE
4 to 6	15 minutes	375°F

	SMOKE TIME	WOOD PELLET FLAVOR
	10 minutes	Maple

FOR THOSE OF us who are used to barbecuing hamburgers, hot dogs, and other meats on the grill, it might be surprising to find fruit in a grilling cookbook. But don't flip to another page just yet—grilled peaches are an easy and tasty treat off of the pellet grill, especially during summer when they're in season. Because they are sweet, tangy, and melt-in-your-mouth soft, pellet-grilled peaches work perfectly as a dessert side, like with vanilla ice cream (though we often eat them on their own).

5 peaches   2 tablespoons olive oil   Ice cream for
                                                     serving (optional)

1. Supply your smoker with wood pellets and follow the manufacturer's specific start-up procedure. Preheat the grill, with the lid closed, to 375°F.

2. Slice the peaches in half and remove the pits. Coat the flesh of the peaches with the olive oil.

3. Once the grill reaches 375°F, place the peaches facedown directly on the grill grate. Cook them for 7 to 10 minutes, or until soft. Remove and serve hot, with ice cream on the side if desired.

COOKING TIP: I recommend checking on the peaches a couple of times throughout the cook, especially if it's your first time. It's easy to overcook them, and if you do, they'll turn into mush.

Honey-Glazed Carrots

SERVES	PREP TIME	SMOKE TEMPERATURE
4 to 6	10 minutes	400°F

	SMOKE TIME	WOOD PELLET FLAVOR
	35 minutes	Apple

AS A KID, carrots were easily my favorite vegetable, the one healthy snack whose subtle sweetness was enough to make me snack on them one after another. This same sweetness is what makes carrots so good for pellet grilling—the sweetness and smoke are a perfect combo. Though the carrots are satisfying on their own, the simple honey glaze in this recipe puts them over the top for the ultimate sweet veggie side.

1½ pounds carrots

2 tablespoons olive oil

Salt

Freshly ground
black pepper

2 tablespoons honey

2 tablespoons
brown sugar

1. Supply your smoker with wood pellets and follow the manufacturer's specific start-up procedure. Preheat the grill, with the lid closed, to 400°F.

2. Peel the carrots and slice them in half lengthwise. Transfer the sliced carrots to a large bowl, drizzle them with the olive oil, and season with salt and pepper. Toss to coat.

3. Place the carrots on the grill and cook them for 20 minutes.

4. At the 20-minute mark, mix the honey and brown sugar in a small microwave-safe bowl. Microwave for 25 seconds and bring the mixture out to the grill.

5. Using a basting brush, baste the carrots with the honey glaze, then flip the carrots and baste the other side.

6. Continue cooking the carrots until they are soft, about 15 more minutes. Remove them from the grill and serve hot.

COOKING TIP: You can also use a grill-safe saucepot to warm the honey glaze directly on the grill. About 5 minutes before basting, mix the ingredients together in the pot and place on the grill to warm through.

Barbecued Roasted Potatoes

SERVES	PREP TIME	SMOKE TEMPERATURE
4 to 6	10 minutes	425°F

	SMOKE TIME	WOOD PELLET FLAVOR
	35 minutes	Hickory

ROASTED POTATOES ARE a simple, tasty side that transfers easily to your pellet grill with very little work and so much more flavor. And here's a time-saving dinner tip to consider: They're also easy to cook alongside a meat. While cooking these potatoes, prep a couple of chicken breasts using the same poultry rub and cook them on the grill next to your baking pan. You should throw them on the grill about 5 minutes after the potatoes, and by the time the potatoes finish, the chicken should reach an internal temperature of 170°F. And there you have it: a full, pellet-grilled meal all in one go.

2 pounds baby red or yellow potatoes

2 tablespoons olive oil

1 batch Poultry Rub (page 151)

1. Supply your smoker with wood pellets and follow the manufacturer's specific start-up procedure. Preheat the grill, with the lid closed, to 425°F.

2. Cut the potatoes into quarters and spread them in an even layer on a baking sheet. Drizzle the potatoes with the olive oil and sprinkle with the poultry rub.

3. Place the baking sheet on the grill and cook until the potatoes are fork-tender, roughly 35 minutes, flipping once halfway through the cooking. Remove them from the grill and serve immediately.

COOKING TIP: Don't borrow baking sheets from your kitchen. Your pellet grill will do a number on your pans. From warping to burned-on sauce, I've retired more than a few pans from cookie duty because of the treatment the grill gave them. These pans are now exclusively for the grill, and I use them for everything from potatoes to ribs without worrying about ruining anything in my kitchen.

Mixed Veggies

SERVES	PREP TIME	SMOKE TEMPERATURE
4 to 6	20 minutes	500°F
	SMOKE TIME	WOOD PELLET FLAVOR
	20 minutes	Alder

FOR THIS DISH. I use a veggie grilling tray or basket—typically a metal tray or basket with small holes punched in it to allow for more airflow to reach the foods inside. Veggie trays help prevent small pieces from falling through the grill grates while mixing. They are some of my most frequently used pellet-grilling tools, and, of course, the most popular dish for them is mixed veggies. This easy dish can combine any of your favorite vegetables and give them a nice wood-fired flavor.

1 zucchini	1 pound baby carrots	Freshly ground black pepper
1 white onion	1 pound snow peas	
1 red bell pepper	3 tablespoons olive oil	1 to 2 tablespoons balsamic glaze
1 green bell pepper	Salt	

1. Supply your smoker with wood pellets and follow the manufacturer's specific start-up procedure. Preheat the grill, with a veggie tray or rimmed baking sheet on the grill grate and the lid closed, to 500°F.

2. Slice the zucchini into rounds, cut the onion into 8 wedges, and slice the peppers into strips. Transfer the sliced veggies to a large mixing bowl, then add the carrots and snow peas. Drizzle the vegetables with the olive oil, add salt and pepper, and toss to combine.

3. Spread the mixed vegetables on the veggie tray (or in a large baking pan) in an even layer. Cook until tender, about 20 minutes, flipping once halfway through. Remove the vegetables from the grill, drizzle with the balsamic glaze, and toss to combine. Serve hot.

COOKING TIP: This recipe is perfect to make using leftover meats as an addition. Throw your leftover cut-up steak or chicken on top of the veggies to create a single-dish meal for the whole family to enjoy.

Pellet-Grilled Corn on the Cob

SERVES	PREP TIME	SMOKE TEMPERATURE
5	10 minutes	425°F
	SMOKE TIME	WOOD PELLET FLAVOR
	10 minutes	Alder

LIKE SO MANY people, I love fresh corn on the cob. (My teeth, not so much, but it's so good I eat it anyway.) During late summer and early fall when corn is in season, I love to stop at local farm stands and pick up a few ears. I cook them up alongside a steak or some chicken drumsticks. Cooking corn on your pellet grill instead of the stove top will give it that signature smoky flavor, and, even better, it'll keep your house cool on those warm summer evenings.

5 ears corn

½ cup (1 stick) butter, melted, divided

Salt

Freshly ground black pepper

1. Supply your smoker with wood pellets and follow the manufacturer's specific start-up procedure. Preheat the grill, with the lid closed, to 425°F.

2. Husk the corn, remove the silk fibers, and baste the corn cobs with half the melted butter. Once the grill reaches 425°F, place the corn on the grill grate and cook for 5 minutes.

3. After 5 minutes, turn the corn and baste the other side with the remaining melted butter. Cook the corn until the ears begin to turn golden brown on the edges, 5 additional minutes. Remove the corn from the grill, add salt and pepper to taste, and serve hot.

COOKING TIP: Leftover grilled corn is amazing in a multitude of uses. A Southwest-style salsa or salad can be sent over the top with this grilled corn's smoky flavor.

Grilled Pineapple Slices

SERVES	PREP TIME	SMOKE TEMPERATURE
4 to 6	10 minutes	400°F

	SMOKE TIME	WOOD PELLET FLAVOR
	10 minutes	Pecan

MY FIRST TIME having grilled pineapple was at a Brazilian steakhouse, and it was something else! The sweet-and-tangy grilled pineapple hit just right with the wood-fired flavor. As with many other new things that I try while eating out, I attempted to create this on my own grill. As it turned out, pellet-grilled sliced pineapple was even better than I expected. The best part of this recipe is that it's so quick and simple, smoking for just 10 minutes and making for an easy side or dessert for your next barbecue.

1 whole pineapple   2 tablespoons olive oil

1. Supply your smoker with wood pellets and follow the manufacturer's specific start-up procedure. Preheat the grill, with the lid closed, to 400°F.

2. Use a large knife to carefully remove the stem, rind, and core from the pineapple. Cut the flesh into ½-inch strips. Coat the pineapple slices with the olive oil.

3. Place the pineapple slices directly on the grill grate. Cook for 5 minutes, then flip and cook for 5 more minutes. Remove from the grill and serve warm.

COOKING TIP: You can also use brown sugar or honey to bring out more of the pineapple's sweetness. Right after pulling them from the grill, sprinkle the slices with 2 or 3 tablespoons of brown sugar or drizzle them with honey.

Grilled Brussels Sprouts

SERVES 4 to 6	PREP TIME 10 minutes	SMOKE TEMPERATURE 375°F
	SMOKE TIME 20 minutes	WOOD PELLET FLAVOR Hickory

BRUSSELS SPROUTS ARE another seemingly ordinary vegetable whose flavor gets cranked up several notches when cooked by wood fire. Most of us right now are probably picturing a bland, boiled sprout that's the last on the plate to be eaten. Rest assured that's not the case here. These Brussels are crisped up and seasoned generously, and cooking them on the wood pellet smoker gives them a spectacular flavor that you just won't get indoors.

1 pound Brussels sprouts	2 tablespoons olive oil	1 batch Poultry Rub (page 151)

1. Supply your smoker with wood pellets and follow the manufacturer's specific start-up procedure. Preheat the grill, with the lid closed, to 375°F.

2. Cut the Brussels sprouts in half lengthwise and spread them on a rimmed baking sheet in an even layer. Drizzle them with the olive oil and sprinkle them with the rub, then toss to combine and spread across the baking sheet again.

3. Place the baking sheet on the grill and cook for 20 minutes, until the Brussels are crispy and browned on the edges. Remove from the grill and serve hot.

COOKING TIP: If you want to set the Brussels sprouts directly on the grill, you can put them on skewers. Thread about six Brussels sprout halves on each skewer and go about the recipe in the same way.

Cheesy Tailgate Potatoes

SERVES	PREP TIME	SMOKE TEMPERATURE
8 to 10	15 minutes	375°F

	SMOKE TIME	WOOD PELLET FLAVOR
	45 minutes	Competition Blend

AS AN OREGON State football season ticketholder, I love to throw home-game tailgate parties throughout football season. When the team goes on the road, I watch from home. And although I may be at home, that doesn't mean I don't go as hard as I would if I were at the game. I typically create an away-game menu, and these cheesy potatoes often make the cut. These are another easy side that I can put on the grill while watching the game, since they don't require any babysitting. This hearty meal goes well with some pork ribs, a couple of IPAs, and a Beaver win!

2 pounds russet potatoes, shredded

1 cup sour cream

1 cup milk

½ cup (1 stick) butter, melted, plus more for greasing the pan

1 (10.5-ounce) can cheddar cheese soup

1 tablespoon garlic salt

2 cups shredded cheddar cheese, divided

1. Supply your smoker with wood pellets and follow the manufacturer's specific start-up procedure. Preheat the grill, with the lid closed, to 375°F.

2. In a large bowl, combine the shredded potatoes, sour cream, milk, melted butter, cheddar cheese soup, garlic salt, and 1½ cups of shredded cheddar. Mix until well combined.

3. Grease a 9-by-13-inch pan with butter. Spread the potato mixture in the pan in an even layer.

4. Place the pan on the grill, cover, and cook for 40 minutes. After 40 minutes, sprinkle the remaining ½ cup of cheddar cheese over the dish. Close the lid and continue cooking the potatoes for 5 additional minutes, until the cheese on top is melted. Remove from the grill and serve immediately.

Barbecued Nachos

SERVES	PREP TIME	SMOKE TEMPERATURE
3 to 5	10 minutes	400°F
	SMOKE TIME	WOOD PELLET FLAVOR
	25 minutes	Competition Blend

EASY. TASTY. MESSY. and most of all cheap—everyone loves nachos, from the littlest kiddos at the table to Grandma and Grandpa. They can be a meal for one or an appetizer for 12, and there are really no rules, so you can add all sorts of toppings. You might be used to making nachos in the oven, but for these, we're going to do the whole process fully on the grill. I call for pulled pork from the Pulled Pork Barbecue Sandwich recipe (page 52) since it usually creates leftovers, but you can really substitute about any shredded meat we cook in this book.

½ bag tortilla chips, plus more for serving

1 (15-ounce) can black beans

2 cups Pulled Pork (page 52) or other leftover shredded barbecued meat

2 cups shredded cheddar cheese

¼ cup sliced jalapeños

1 cup shredded lettuce

½ cup Smoked Salsa (page 139) or store-bought salsa

1 (2.5-ounce) can sliced olives

¼ cup sour cream

1. Supply your smoker with wood pellets and follow the manufacturer's specific start-up procedure. Preheat the grill, with the lid closed, to 400°F.

2. Arrange a layer of tortilla chips at the bottom of a large cast-iron skillet or baking pan. Cover them with the beans, pork, cheddar cheese, and jalapeños.

3. Once the grill reaches 400°F, place the skillet at the center of the grill. Cover and cook for 25 minutes.

4. Remove the skillet from the grill and top with the shredded lettuce, salsa, olives, and sour cream. Serve immediately, with additional chips on the side.

COOKING TIP: For extra flavor, swap out the tortilla chips for Doritos. My mom does this, and I have to say it's unbelievable. I don't feel one bit healthy when I make this change, but tastewise it's definitely worth it.

Smoked Mac and Cheese

SERVES	PREP TIME	SMOKE TEMPERATURE
8 to 10	15 minutes	375°F, then 180°F
	SMOKE TIME	WOOD PELLET FLAVOR
	30 minutes	Hickory

MANY OF US grew up on macaroni and cheese, but, fortunately or unfortunately, the kind I had was always from the blue box. That stuff brings back childhood summer memories of visiting my aunt Jeanie, whose exquisite cuisine was often decked out with some sliced hot dogs or hamburger meat if we were getting really fancy. This near-daily vacation lunch went amazing with a drink of hose water and the filling from an Oreo, but as I've aged, it somehow doesn't hit the same. To bring back some of that mac and cheese nostalgia, make this genuinely delicious smoked take on your pellet grill.

1 pound elbow macaroni

4 tablespoons butter

1 cup milk

4 ounces cream cheese

1 cup cheddar cheese, shredded

Salt

Freshly ground black pepper

1. Supply your smoker with wood pellets and follow the manufacturer's specific start-up procedure. Preheat the grill, with a cast-iron skillet and pot on the grate and the lid closed, to 375°F.

2. Meanwhile, cook the elbow macaroni in the cast-iron pot on the grill, according to the package instructions, but do not adjust your grill's temperature at any time. (If you prefer, you can cook the macaroni on the stove top instead.) When the pasta is ready, drain it and set aside.

3. When the grill reaches 375°F, add the butter, milk, and cream cheese to the cast-iron skillet. Stir until melted and combined, then reduce the grill temperature to 180°F. Stir in the macaroni.

4. Add the shredded cheese, salt, and pepper to the macaroni mixture. Mix well, cover, and allow to smoke at 180°F for 30 minutes. Remove from the grill and serve immediately.

MARIONBERRY PIE ★ 136

BREADS, SNACKS, AND DESSERTS

ONE OF the ways the pellet grill sets itself apart from every other grill on the market is its ability to bake. Actually, pellet-grill baking can often produce better results than baking traditional style in an oven. The indirect, wood-fired heat is the most versatile way to cook outdoors, and that includes treats, snacks, and other baked goods and desserts. Breads and cookies are just the beginning of what you can do—fruit pies, smoked cheeses and nuts, and cinnamon rolls are all possible. If you can do it in an oven, most likely you can do it on a pellet grill.

BAKING IN THE BACKYARD

So many foods turn out nicely when baked on the grill, but those that lend themselves to smoky flavors are particularly great. Wood-Fired Beer Bread (page 126) and Margherita Pizza (page 130) take on the smoke tremendously well, offering a whole new flavor profile for otherwise familiar foods. And just like pork and poultry cooked with sweet rubs and sauces, sweet baked goods are fantastic cooked the same way on a wood pellet grill.

Definitely make sure you have specific baking gear that you use strictly for the grill. You'll save time lugging stuff back and forth from the kitchen, and on the off-chance something gets damaged, your kitchen will still be stocked. Though most bakeware will work, the grill is a totally different environment from your oven. For one, I would avoid glassware, since it can't withstand the high temperatures of a grill. If for some reason direct flame reaches your glass pan, you'll likely be in the market for a new one.

DESSERT TIME

Now is when we turn to our sweet tooth. Smoke and fire vibes well with fruits and sweets, and they are super easy to prepare on the grill. Cookies, cakes, and pies are awesome on the grill, and at this point I prefer them cooked that way. Marilyn's Cinnamon Rolls (page 134) and Easy Monkey Bread (page 127) are treats that most might think are reserved for the oven, but with this chapter, they'll see new life on your pellet grill.

A cast-iron skillet is your friend when making pellet-grilled desserts, since it can withstand a lot of direct heat. These skillets and metal roasting pans work wonders for breads, cakes, and pies. Again, steer away from glass-ware, since it can't handle as much heat.

NUTS AND CHEESE

Nuts and cheeses taste totally different when they're smoked. The added flavor is unmatchable, and as a bonus the smoking can be done quickly. Smoked nuts and cheeses make amazing appetizers at parties or as holiday gifts for coworkers. Fancy nuts and cheese are always part of gift baskets, so why not take it to the next level by smoking them yourself?

Nuts are a very easy smoke and can be done with little effort, so they're a good project for a beginner (see Smoked Mixed Nuts, page 131). Smoking cheese, on the other hand, is slightly more difficult, though still relatively easy because of the ability to control temperature in a pellet grill. The trick to smoking cheese is simple: Keep it from getting too hot (see Smoked Cheddar, page 138). If your cheese does get too hot and melts, it's not inedible, but it's probably best suited to be shredded for nachos or tacos.

|||||||||||||||||||||||||||||||| **PRO TIPS** ||||||||||||||||||||||||||||||||||

→ Baking on a grill is a lot like baking in your oven, except for the fire. The fire can cause hot spots or a quicker cook on the bottom than on the top, leading to uneven baking. This is not a huge problem if you're willing to work with it. Using a lower temperature and rotating your dish intermittently during the cook is about all you need to do to ensure even cooking.

→ For smoked nuts and cheese, I recommend using a tube smoker. These small cold smokers use additional barbecue wood pellets to generate additional smoke. I use the A-MAZE-N Tube Smoker, available at Walmart and online.

→ Try to avoid using your regular kitchen tools and supplies on the grill. Many of these products are not built for the fire, high heat, and other aspects of a barbecue grill; plus, barbecues are dirty. No one wants to keep the rubber spatula you left lying out on the grill.

Wood-Fired Beer Bread

SERVES	PREP TIME	SMOKE TEMPERATURE
6 to 8	10 minutes	350°F
	SMOKE TIME	WOOD PELLET FLAVOR
	1 hour	Hickory

BAKING ON THE grill is something that we all should do more of. Wood firing gives baked goods a depth of flavor that you just can't get from the oven. One of my favorite things to bake on the grill is bread—it has a subtle smoky flavor that is hard to beat. The thing that puts a lot of people off of baking bread is that it can be difficult and time-consuming to make. Beer bread gets that obstacle out of the way. The yeast from the beer helps the bread rise quickly, eliminating much of the work and waiting around involved with traditional bread.

3 cups all-purpose flour, sifted

3 tablespoons granulated sugar

1 tablespoon baking powder

1 teaspoon salt

1 (12-ounce) beer (see cooking tip after the recipe)

¼ cup (½ stick) butter, melted, plus more for greasing the pan

1. Supply your smoker with wood pellets and follow the manufacturer's specific start-up procedure. Preheat the grill, with the lid closed, to 350°F.

2. In a large mixing bowl, combine the flour, sugar, baking powder, and salt, and stir to incorporate. Pour in the beer and stir to combine. The mixture will be much looser than your typical bread dough, almost like a batter in texture.

3. Grease a 9-by-5-inch loaf pan with butter. and evenly pour the bread mixture into the pan. Pour the melted butter on top of the mixture.

4. Place the loaf pan on the grill, cover, and cook until golden brown on top, about 1 hour. Let the bread rest for 5 to 10 minutes before removing from the pan. Slice and serve warm.

COOKING TIP: For different flavor, play with the beer that you use. Light and domestic beers are the easy go-to choices, but as someone who lives in the land of the craft brew, I can't resist trying all different kinds of beers in my bread.

Easy Monkey Bread

SERVES	PREP TIME	SMOKE TEMPERATURE
6 to 8	15 minutes	350°F
	SMOKE TIME	WOOD PELLET FLAVOR
	40 minutes	Maple

THE FIRST TIME I heard I was about to have monkey bread, I had no idea what my wife was getting me into. Luckily, I was pleasantly surprised. I had no idea a clump of biscuits could be so good. This monkey bread is a genuinely easy dessert treat that can be made with only a few ingredients and some short prep that even kids can help with.

½ cup granulated sugar

2 teaspoons cinnamon

2 (16-ounce) canisters store-bought biscuit dough (such as Pillsbury)

1 cup (2 sticks) butter, melted, plus more for greasing the pan

1 cup packed brown sugar

1. Supply your smoker with wood pellets and follow the manufacturer's specific start-up procedure. Preheat the grill, with the lid closed, to 350°F.

2. Combine the granulated sugar and cinnamon in a gallon-size resealable plastic bag.

3. Remove the biscuit dough from the canisters and cut each biscuit round into quarters. Add the quarters to the plastic bag with the sugar and cinnamon, and shake well to coat the pieces.

4. Generously grease a Bundt pan with butter. Add the sugar-coated biscuit pieces to the pan and spread evenly to ensure even cooking.

5. In a medium bowl, combine the melted butter and the brown sugar and stir to incorporate. Pour this mixture evenly over the biscuit pieces in the Bundt pan.

6. Place the Bundt pan on the grill, cover, and cook until golden brown on top, about 40 minutes. Once finished, let the monkey bread rest for 5 minutes, then flip the Bundt pan onto a tray. Slice or tear apart and enjoy immediately.

Homestyle Rolls

SERVES	PREP TIME	SMOKE TEMPERATURE
8 to 12	45 minutes, plus 1½ hours rising	400°F
		WOOD PELLET FLAVOR
	SMOKE TIME 15 minutes	Maple

HOMEMADE DINNER ROLLS are the best. They take me back to holiday meals with family. Not much is better than having a nice, warm, fresh-made roll smothered in butter. Adding a little hardwood fire flavor to your rolls just makes them all the tastier. Use this recipe at your next family dinner to wow the rest of the table.

2 (¼-ounce) packages active dry yeast

¼ cup lukewarm water

1 cup milk, warmed to room temperature

2 large eggs

4½ cups all-purpose flour, sifted

1 teaspoon salt

¼ cup canola oil

Butter, for greasing the pan, plus more for serving

1. In a large bowl, combine the yeast and water and mix well. Add the milk and eggs, whisking with a fork until fully incorporated. It's important that the water and milk are at room temperature so the yeast will activate.

2. Use a wooden spoon to mix in the flour and salt. Add the canola oil and stir to incorporate. The dough should be overall cohesive but sticky.

3. Transfer the dough to a baking sheet or other work surface and knead. To knead, push down on the dough with the ball of your palm and fold the dough over on itself, then push down again and repeat. Kneading should take 7 or 8 minutes, and, once finished, the dough should look smooth and no longer be sticky.

4. Cover the dough with plastic wrap and let it rise until it's just about doubled in size, roughly 1 hour.

5. After the dough has doubled in size, punch down on the dough to deflate it. Then cover it back up with plastic wrap and allow it to rise for 5 more minutes. Meanwhile, grease a 9-by-13-inch baking pan with butter.

6. Divide the dough into 12 equal-size pieces and shape into spheres. Put them into the greased baking pan, spaced evenly apart. Cover again with plastic wrap and let them rise one last time, until the rolls have nearly doubled in size, about 30 minutes.

7. While the dough is rising for the last time, supply your smoker with wood pellets and follow the manufacturer's specific start-up procedure. Preheat the grill, with the lid closed, to 400°F.

8. Place the baking pan of rolls on the grill, cover, and allow to cook until golden brown, roughly 10 to 15 minutes. Remove the rolls from the grill and serve immediately with butter.

COOKING TIP: If you're able to, set out your eggs early, allowing them to reach room temperature before mixing them into the dough. This will help keep the yeast warm, expediting the rising process.

Margherita Pizza

SERVES 4 to 6	PREP TIME 10 minutes	SMOKE TEMPERATURE 425°F
	SMOKE TIME 10 minutes	WOOD PELLET FLAVOR Hickory

IN MY TOTALLY impartial opinion, the best pizzas are made on a wood pellet grill. Even store-bought party pizzas can be taken to the next level with that wood-fired flavor. As pellet grilling expanded in the early 2010s, Traeger Grills became a popular way to cook take-and-bake pizzas (take-and-bake pizza franchises were even some of Traeger's early dealers). Needless to say, I have had my fair share of pizza from a pellet grill, and my favorites are always the ones we build and customize ourselves.

1 tablespoon cornmeal

1 (14-ounce) store-bought pizza dough (I use Pillsbury, available at most grocery stores)

½ cup pizza sauce

1 cup shredded mozzarella cheese

1 Roma tomato, sliced

½ cup fresh basil leaves, sliced or torn

2 garlic cloves, minced

1 tablespoon olive oil

1. Supply your smoker with wood pellets and follow the manufacturer's specific start-up procedure. Preheat the grill, with the lid closed, to 425°F.

2. Sprinkle the cornmeal onto a baking sheet or pizza pan to prevent the dough from sticking. Use your hands to press the pizza dough into the baking sheet, 10 to 12 inches in diameter.

3. Spread the sauce evenly on top of the pizza dough, followed by the cheese, tomato, basil, and garlic. Drizzle the pizza with olive oil.

4. Place the baking sheet on the grill and cover. Cook until the cheese is melted and the bottom of the pizza is golden brown, approximately 12 minutes.

5. Remove the pizza from the grill and serve immediately.

COOKING TIP: If you cook pizza often, a pizza stone is a quality investment. The stone transfers heat equally and will hold up to your grill much better than a regular baking sheet.

Smoked Mixed Nuts

SERVES	PREP TIME	SMOKE TEMPERATURE
6 to 8	5 minutes	180°F
	SMOKE TIME	WOOD PELLET FLAVOR
	1 hour	Mesquite

ONE OF THE best things about pellet grilling is that you can take the most ordinary of foods, give it a quick smoke, and turn it into something completely different. By that measure, smoked snacks are some of the most irresistible smoked foods. Smoked mixed nuts are an easy way to kick a little life into your next party—it's a simple process with a huge payoff. After you try this technique, just wait and see if you'll ever be willing to eat them straight out of the can again.

1 (12-ounce) can mixed nuts (Planters brand is my go-to)

1. Supply your smoker with wood pellets and follow the manufacturer's specific start-up procedure. Preheat the grill, with the lid closed, to 180°F.

2. Spread the nuts evenly on a rimmed baking sheet and set directly on the grill.

3. Cover and smoke at 180°F for 1 hour, stirring at 20 minutes and 40 minutes to ensure even smoking.

4. After an hour, remove the nuts from the grill. You could technically eat these right away, but to ensure the best smoky flavor, wait at least 1 hour (or ideally as long as 24 hours) before serving.

COOKING TIP: This same technique can be used for many smoked snacks. My (and my kids') favorite is Cheez-Its. I smoke the crackers the same way I do the mixed nuts, and they're great every time—I just have to hope the kids don't eat them all before I get a chance.

Grill Master Chocolate Chip Cookies

SERVES	PREP TIME	SMOKE TEMPERATURE
10 to 12	25 minutes	350°F
	SMOKE TIME	WOOD PELLET FLAVOR
	10 minutes	Pecan

YOU MIGHT BE surprised if I told you the sweet tooth of an expert griller knows no bounds. But think for a second: Why do you think everything is covered in sweet barbecue sauces and other sugary spice mixes? To feed my own sweet tooth, beyond my normal grilling, I reach for chocolate. And there isn't any chocolate on the grill I love more than chocolate chip cookies.

½ cup (1 stick) butter

1 cup granulated sugar

1 cup brown sugar

2 large eggs

1 teaspoon
vanilla extract

2¼ cups
all-purpose flour

1 teaspoon baking soda

1 teaspoon salt

2 cups semi-sweet
chocolate chips

1. Microwave the butter in a medium microwave-safe bowl (or in a medium pot over medium-high heat on the stove top) until melted. Once the butter is melted, mix in the granulated and brown sugars, eggs, and vanilla until well combined.

2. In a separate medium bowl, stir together the flour, baking soda, and salt.

3. Add the wet mixture to the dry mixture and stir well, until no dry spots remain. Stir in the chocolate chips.

4. Supply your smoker with wood pellets and follow the manufacturer's specific start-up procedure. Preheat the grill, with the lid closed, to 350°F.

5. Line a baking sheet with aluminum foil. Drop about 1½-inch spoonfuls of cookie dough onto the baking sheet, leaving about 2 inches between the cookies to allow for spreading.

6. Place the baking sheet on the grill, cover, and cook until the cookies are golden-brown, 10 to 12 minutes.

7. Remove from the grill and use a spatula to transfer the cookies to wire racks to cool. Serve warm.

COOKING TIP: When baking on a pellet grill, beware of hot spots. I know my grill's hot spots, but I usually don't spend time worrying about them. That's different with baking since hot spots can cause the bottom of your baked goods to burn. If you notice a heavy hot spot, to prevent burning, bake at a lower temperature and turn your baked goods halfway through.

Marilyn's Cinnamon Rolls

SERVES	PREP TIME	SMOKE TEMPERATURE
8 to 12	1 hour, plus 1½ hours rising	400°F

	SMOKE TIME	WOOD PELLET FLAVOR
	15 minutes	Maple

CINNAMON ROLLS WERE one of my all-time favorite treats growing up. When I was young, my parents would bring them home from our local grocery store, Roth's—the same store where I worked at all through college (and also a pellet-grill dealer). I thought Roth's had the best cinnamon rolls around, but all that changed once I had ones made by my mother-in-law, Marilyn. As with so many things, the homemade version is the best. Though Marilyn's own cinnamon rolls are hard to replicate, I do my best using my pellet grill. I cook my cinnamon rolls in my cast-iron skillet, which carries a more even heat.

2 (¼ ounce) packages active dry yeast

¼ cup lukewarm water

1 cup milk, warmed to room temperature

2 large eggs

4½ cups all-purpose flour, sifted

1 teaspoon salt

¼ cup canola oil

2 tablespoons butter, at room temperature, plus more for greasing and serving

2 cups brown sugar

1 tablespoon cinnamon

1. In a large bowl, combine the yeast and lukewarm water and mix well. Add the milk and eggs, whisking with a fork until fully incorporated. It's important that the water and milk are at room temperature so that the yeast will activate.

2. Use a wooden spoon to mix in the flour and salt. Add the canola oil and stir to incorporate. The dough should be cohesive but sticky and somewhat shaggy.

3. Transfer the dough mixture to a baking sheet or other work surface and knead. To knead, push down on the dough with the ball of your palm and fold the dough over on itself, then push down again and repeat. Kneading this way should take about 7 or 8 minutes. Once the dough is fully kneaded, it should look smooth and be on the shinier side, and it should no longer be sticky.

4. Cover the dough with plastic wrap and let it rise until it's just about double its original size, roughly 1 hour.

5. After the dough has doubled in size, punch down on it to deflate it. Then cover it back up with plastic wrap and allow it to rise for 5 more minutes. Meanwhile, grease a 12-inch cast-iron skillet with butter.

6. Roll the dough into a square shape as best as you can, about ¼ inch thick.

7. Spread 2 tablespoons of butter evenly over the dough. Sprinkle the brown sugar and cinnamon on top of the butter, completely covering the surface of the dough.

8. Cut the dough lengthwise into 8 equal strips and roll each strip into a spiral roll. Put each roll into your greased cast-iron skillet.

9. Cover the rolls in the skillet with plastic wrap and allow them to rise one last time, until roughly doubled in size, about 30 minutes.

10. Supply your smoker with wood pellets and follow the manufacturer's specific start-up procedure. Preheat the grill, with the lid closed, to 400°F.

11. Place the skillet of rolls on the grill, cover, and allow them to cook for 10 to 15 minutes, or until golden brown on top. Remove the rolls from the grill and serve immediately, with butter.

COOKING TIP: For an even sweeter cinnamon roll, top with vanilla or cream cheese frosting. Also, depending on your spice preference, you can increase or reduce the amount of cinnamon by ½ teaspoon.

Marionberry Pie

SERVES 8 to 12	PREP TIME 25 minutes	SMOKE TEMPERATURE 350°F
	SMOKE TIME 1 hour	WOOD PELLET FLAVOR Alder

ALONG WITH THE pellet grill, one of the more interesting things to come out of Marion County, Oregon, is the marionberry. This breed of blackberry is extremely sweet and flavorful and was developed by Oregon State University in Marion County. It is now widespread, and you can find marionberry treats everywhere. Marionberry farms are all over Oregon; some good family friends, Tom and Becky Espe, actually own one. Growing up, I would often go out with family and friends to pick berries to enjoy at home. The berries, plus a pellet grill sitting on my parents' porch, resulted in the first dessert I remember being cooked on a grill: a marionberry pie. Here's my time-tested recipe.

6 cups marion-
berries, washed
(blackberries are a
suitable substitute)

1 cup granulated sugar

5 tablespoons
cornstarch

1 tablespoon freshly
squeezed lemon juice

1 (14-ounce) package
store-bought refrige-
rated pie crusts,
softened according
to package direc-
tions (the package
should come with
2 pie crusts)

1 large egg

1. Supply your smoker with wood pellets and follow the manufacturer's specific start-up procedure. Preheat the grill, with the lid closed, to 350°F.

2. Spread the marionberries on a paper towel. Use a second paper towel to pat them dry.

3. In a large mixing bowl, combine the marionberries, sugar, cornstarch, and lemon juice. Stir gently to incorporate.

4. Roll the first pie crust into a 13-inch round and transfer it to a 9-inch pie tin. Pour the marionberry mixture into the crust-lined tin.

5. Roll the remaining pie crust into an 11-inch round and center it over the berry mixture in the tin. Tuck the crust edges under and use the tines of a fork to crimp the edges to create a seal. Use a knife to make a few air vents in the top crust.

6. In a small bowl, beat the egg until white and yoke are combined. Use a basting brush to brush the egg wash across the top pie crust.

7. Place the pie on the grill grate and bake, covered, for 1 hour, or until golden brown on top. Let the pie rest for at least 2 hours before serving.

COOKING TIP: After serving, cover your leftover pie and keep refrigerated. The pie will stay fresh for up to a week.

Smoked Cheddar

SERVES	PREP TIME	SMOKE TEMPERATURE
10 to 12	5 minutes	180°F *(if your grill has a "Smoke" or lower setting, use it)*
	SMOKE TIME	
	1½ hours	WOOD PELLET FLAVOR
		Hickory

IT MIGHT SOUND unusual, but smoked cheese is something that you just have to try on your pellet grill—you won't be disappointed. Smoked cheddar is especially popular around the holidays when it's coldest and easiest to cook, since the smoking needs to happen at a lower temperature to prevent the cheese from melting. Smoke some for your next holiday party or even to give as gifts to friends and family on Christmas Day.

1 (2-pound) block cheddar cheese

1. Supply your smoker with wood pellets and follow the manufacturer's specific start-up procedure. Preheat the grill, with the lid closed, to 180°F.

2. Spread a layer of ice on a rimmed baking sheet and set it directly on the lower grate of the grill (assuming the grill has two or more racks). If your grill has a single rack, set the baking sheet on the drain pan and place the grill grate above it.

3. Quarter the block of cheese, slicing lengthwise, and put it on another baking sheet. Set the baking sheet with the cheese on the upper grill grate, above the ice. Smoke for 1½ hours.

4. After smoking, remove the cheese from the grill. Refrigerate overnight before serving.

COOKING TIP: Smoked cheddar is so good, but I won't lie, it's very difficult to keep it from melting. I rarely try it on days when the temperature is above freezing. Make sure to use your grill's lowest heat setting, and don't skip the ice. I'd suggest cooking at night to avoid sunlight and the heat of the day. And, if you can, prop your grill's lid open about half an inch to allow even more heat to escape.

Smoked Salsa

SERVES	PREP TIME	SMOKE TEMPERATURE
4 to 6	15 minutes	180°F
	SMOKE TIME	WOOD PELLET FLAVOR
	1 hour	Mesquite

SOME OF THE things we cook on the grill will gain a subtle flavor from the wood, but it won't be fundamentally different than what you're used to eating prepared another way. Salsa is not one of those things. Smoking your salsa ingredients before blending will give your salsa a totally different, wood-fired flavor that will have people asking how on earth you worked your magic.

3 beefsteak tomatoes

1 white onion

2 jalapeños

1 green bell pepper

1 tablespoon olive oil

1 bunch cilantro

3 garlic cloves

1 lime

Salt

Freshly ground
black pepper

Tortilla chips, for serving

1. Supply your smoker with wood pellets and follow the manufacturer's specific start-up procedure. Preheat the grill, with the lid closed, to 180°F.

2. Slice in half the tomatoes, onion, jalapeños, and bell pepper, removing the peel from the onion and the seeds, stem, and pith from the peppers.

3. Spread out the cut vegetables on a baking tray and drizzle them with the olive oil. Place the tray on the grill, cover, and smoke for 1 hour.

4. While the vegetables are smoking, cut the stems off the cilantro, mince the garlic, and juice the lime.

5. After 1 hour of smoking, remove the baking tray with the tomatoes, onion, and peppers from the grill and transfer the contents to a blender. Add the cilantro leaves, garlic, and lime juice. Season with salt and pepper to taste.

6. Blend the salsa until smooth. Serve with tortilla chips. Refrigerate leftover salsa for up to a week in an airtight container.

COOKING TIP: For a spicier salsa, reserve around half the jalapeño seeds and add them back into the mixture just before blending.

PULLED PORK BARBECUE SANDWICHES ★ 52

SAUCES, RUBS, AND RELISHES

RUBS, SAUCES, and relishes provide the base seasoning to many of the dishes in this book. With that said, the great thing about a pellet grill is that you don't need the most powerful spice or sauce to make the meal special—the grill is what makes the flavors really come to life. These basic recipes are all meant to work with the pellet-grilling technique to help bring out the best flavors in your food without overpowering what the smoke brings to the table.

HOMEMADE IS ALWAYS BEST

The best sauces, spices, rubs, and relishes are the ones you make at home. The ones you find at the store are often overflavored, oversalted, or otherwise overprocessed. They also sometimes come with artificial flavors, like liquid smoke, which our grill should provide for us. There are some good ones out there that complement dishes well, but I prefer to make a lot of the basics at home. Making your own sauces, rubs, and relishes allows you to personalize them to fit your taste and to work best with your grill.

Making your own seasonings is also a great way to save money. Most of the recipes in this chapter use items you likely already have in your cupboard—and the ones you don't have are things you can easily find at the store. My recipes are a great starting point, but you can use these basic spices and ingredients in new combinations to invent your own rubs, relishes, and sauces.

➡ All the recipes in this book can be doubled or tripled to build large batches or to store. The relishes and sauces should be used within about a week for best results. Dry spice rubs can keep longer, stored in an airtight container for a few months.

➡ Sweet sauces and rubs work perfectly for pork and poultry. Brown sugar is a base for many of these recipes, and it's a great base to use to experiment with your own sweet spice blends.

➡ Spicy and herby flavors work amazingly for just about all meats—just be sparing so you don't overpower the meat's flavor.

➡ Your sauces can all be cooked on the grill: Pull out the cast iron and cook them as you would on the stove top. As long as you're careful and stir often, you can even close the grill lid and smoke them for a short time.

➡ Don't cook your sauces over too high a heat. Doing so can cause them to burn, and no one wants burnt barbecue.

➡ In the same vein as the previous tip, your sauce will burn, rather than caramelizing, on the meat at temperatures of 350°F and above. If you are cooking the meat after brushing on the sauce, stay low in temperature and don't go for too long.

Slightly Spicy Barbecue Sauce

beef, chicken, pork, turkey

PREP TIME	COOK TIME
10 minutes	10 minutes

A GOOD BARBECUE sauce is a must-have for any griller. From chicken to pulled pork to ribs, barbecue sauce is a staple to have on hand to make countless recipes, including several in this book. Personally, I like my sauce to be sweet, but it also needs to have a little kick, so that's just what I did with this recipe. The underlying spiciness in a good sauce works to add depth to the flavor of just about any meat. This sauce does exactly that: a spicy-sweet combination that will pair with any meat or dish created on your pellet grill.

2 tablespoons olive oil

½ white onion, finely diced

1 (8-ounce) can tomato sauce

½ cup brown sugar

¼ cup white vinegar

1½ tablespoons Worcestershire sauce

3 teaspoons chili powder

¼ teaspoon dry mustard

2 teaspoons salt

2 teaspoons freshly ground black pepper

1. In a medium saucepan over medium-high heat on the stove top, heat the olive oil. Once it's hot, add the onion and sauté until tender and semitranslucent, about 5 minutes.

2. Add the tomato sauce, brown sugar, white vinegar, Worcestershire sauce, chili powder, dry mustard, salt, and pepper, whisking until well incorporated. Heat the mixture until it reaches a boil, stirring constantly.

3. Remove the sauce from the heat and brush it on your favorite meat. Keep extra sauce refrigerated for up to a week.

COOKING TIP: This recipe can always be cooked right on the grill! Use a cast-iron skillet or saucepan and follow the same instructions. If you close the lid every now and again while cooking, you might even get a hint of smoky flavor.

Teriyaki Sauce

beef, chicken, pork

PREP TIME	COOK TIME
5 minutes	5 minutes

AFTER I RELEASED my previous book, *Master the Wood Pellet Grill*, I was surprised at how popular some of the teriyaki recipes turned out to be. In reality, it should have been obvious. Teriyaki flavor is so versatile and works especially well to complement chicken and pork. This recipe is a variation on the teriyaki marinade from that book. This version, made into an awesome sauce, will work wonders on your dishes, making your next chicken skewers the talk of the town.

1 cup water

⅓ cup soy sauce

¼ cup brown sugar

1 tablespoon Worcestershire sauce

2 garlic cloves, minced

2 tablespoons cornstarch

¼ cup cold water

1. In a saucepan set over medium-high heat on the stove top, combine the water, soy sauce, brown sugar, Worcestershire sauce, and garlic. Whisk to combine and allow the mixture to heat through.

2. In a small bowl, mix together the cornstarch and cold water. Once the soy sauce mixture is hot, add the cornstarch mixture and whisk to incorporate. Stir the sauce frequently, until thickened. Remove the sauce from the heat and brush it on your favorite meat. Keep extra sauce refrigerated for up to a week.

COOKING TIP: One of my favorite uses for this teriyaki sauce is for smoked pork tenderloins. Try it with the Smoked and Seared Pork Tenderloins (page 56). Coat the tenderloins with sauce right after cooking for a spectacular sweet-and-tangy dish.

Beef Marinade

beef, bison, lamb

PREP TIME: 5 minutes

A GREAT MARINADE can turn the humblest cut of beef into something spectacular. Even giving a steak a short bath in a flavorful marinade will intensify the end product so much more than if you had just put it straight on the grill. This marinade amplifies the flavor of the beef itself while also packing it with a garlic-pepper punch.

½ cup water

½ cup soy sauce

¼ cup olive oil

¼ cup Worcestershire sauce

2 garlic cloves, sliced

2 tablespoons freshly ground black pepper

1. In a small mixing bowl, combine the water, soy sauce, olive oil, Worcestershire sauce, garlic, and pepper. Mix everything together until well incorporated.

2. Let the meat sit in the mixture for at least 30 minutes. Store any unused marinade in an airtight container in the refrigerator for up to a week.

COOKING TIP: Thirty minutes is the minimum, but you can marinate meats anywhere up to 24 hours. As I mentioned, even a short marinade will give the meat a lot more flavor.

Butter Poultry Injectable

chicken, duck, turkey

PREP TIME	COOK TIME
5 minutes	5 minutes

BUTTER AND BARBECUE go together great. Sticks of butter are used regularly when searing steaks, basting turkeys, and grilling fish. When grilling, one of my favorite ways to use butter is with poultry. Rubbing a bird with butter, including under the skin, gives it incredible moisture and buttery flavor. To punch that flavor right into your poultry, you can use an injector, available at most grocery stores. Injecting the bird will take it to the next level of buttery, juicy goodness.

1 cup (2 sticks) butter

1 tablespoon salt

1½ teaspoons garlic powder

1 teaspoon onion powder

1. Heat the butter on the stove top over medium heat, until melted. Once the butter is melted, stir in the salt, garlic powder, and onion powder.

2. Use a meat injector to inject the liquid under the skin, throughout the breasts and legs.

COOKING TIP: This injectable can be used for a mop as well. Use the heated butter mixture to baste your turkeys and chickens.

Smoked Jalapeño Relish

beef, chicken, pork

PREP TIME	SMOKE TEMPERATURE
15 minutes	180°F
SMOKE TIME	WOOD PELLET FLAVOR
1 hour	Mesquite

RELISHES ARE AMAZING sides to serve with all sorts of dishes. Though most of us are used to a standard dill pickle relish, a jalapeño relish is all sorts of awesome. The heat element is perfect and works as a savory condiment or dip for all kinds of meats and veggies. As with so many foods, jalapeño relish tastes so much better with smoke, so we pump some into this recipe.

1 pound jalapeños

1 tablespoon olive oil

3 garlic cloves

¼ cup white vinegar

2 teaspoons salt

1 teaspoon freshly ground black pepper

1. Supply your smoker with wood pellets and follow the manufacturer's specific start-up procedure. Preheat the grill, with the lid closed, to 180°F.

2. Slice the jalapeños in half lengthwise, removing the stem, seeds, and pith.

3. Set the cut jalapeños on an aluminum tray or baking sheet and drizzle them with the olive oil.

4. Place the baking sheet on the grill and smoke them for 1 hour. Remove the tray from the grill. (At this point, you're done with the grilling part of the recipe.)

5. In a blender, pulse the garlic into small pieces. Once the garlic is chopped up, add the smoked jalapeños and blend until the peppers are in small pieces.

6. Add the vinegar, salt, and pepper to the blender. Blend all the ingredients together, until the jalapeño pieces are minced.

7. Serve the relish with chips or use it as a topping for your next hot dog or burger. In a sealed container, it should last up to a week refrigerated.

COOKING TIP: Make the relish a day ahead and store it overnight for a smokier flavor.

Pork Rub

chicken, pork, turkey

PREP TIME: 5 minutes

A GREAT SWEET-AND-SALTY pork rub is a must-have for not only pork but poultry as well. This recipe is on the sweet side and is a great complement to ribs or a large pork butt. Check the tip after the recipe for directions to turn this rub into an injectable.

¼ cup brown sugar

1 teaspoon kosher salt

1 teaspoon garlic powder

1 teaspoon onion powder

1 teaspoon freshly ground black pepper

½ teaspoon cayenne pepper

½ teaspoon paprika

½ teaspoon smoked paprika

→ In a small mixing bowl, combine the brown sugar, salt, garlic powder, onion powder, black pepper, cayenne, paprika, and smoked paprika. Mix all the spices until well incorporated. Store any unused rub in a resealable bag or airtight container.

COOKING TIP: This rub can be used to make an injectable as well. Pour the spices into a coffee filter and tie it off using string or butcher's twine. Steep in boiling water, like a tea, for about 20 minutes. Use the steeped liquid as an injectable for poultry or pork.

Poultry Rub

beef, chicken, Cornish hen, turkey, vegetables

PREP TIME: 5 minutes

POULTRY. AND CHICKEN especially, is a mainstay on my grill. I've had it on the grill since a very young age, and I continue to cook it to this day, often multiple times a week. There are a lot of different poultry rub recipes out there, but this one leans deeper into the flavors of garlic and onion than other varieties you might find. It works for all cuts, but I especially love this seasoning on chicken breasts and tenders.

3 tablespoons
   kosher salt

2 tablespoons freshly
   ground black pepper

1 tablespoon
   garlic powder

1 tablespoon
   granulated sugar

1 tablespoon
   brown sugar

½ tablespoon
   minced onion

1 teaspoon cumin

→ In a small mixing bowl, combine the salt, pepper, garlic powder, granulated sugar, brown sugar, onion, and cumin. Mix all the spices together until well incorporated. Store any unused rub in a resealable bag or airtight container.

COOKING TIP: This rub also goes well with beef. The garlic and onion flavors will complement your red meat well—it's one of my favorites for steak.

Blackened Cajun Rub

chicken, duck, sausage, seafood

PREP TIME: 5 minutes

BLACKENED SEASONING IS a close cousin of Cajun and Creole seasoning blends. This seasoning is very similar to my own Cajun rub, but it doesn't use as many of the herbs that we associate with Cajun flavors. Because it uses a pared-down, simpler assortment of herbs, this rub is cheaper (and quicker) to make.

1 tablespoon kosher salt

1 tablespoon garlic powder

1 tablespoon paprika

1 tablespoon onion powder

1 tablespoon freshly ground black pepper

½ tablespoon cayenne pepper

½ tablespoon onion powder

→ In a small mixing bowl, combine the salt, garlic powder, paprika, onion powder, black pepper, cayenne, and onion powder. Mix all the spices together until well incorporated. Store any unused rub in a resealable bag or airtight container.

COOKING TIP: Blackened Cajun Rub is awesome for seafood. Use this for everything from catfish to fried oysters cooked on the stove top.

Brisket Rub

beef, bison

PREP TIME: 5 minutes

I'M GOING TO let you in on a little secret: Most of the world's best smokers use simply salt and pepper to season their brisket. Brisket is one of those meats that, because of the cut and the way you cook it, carries much of its own flavor. While I'm not telling you as a beginner to go out and start using only salt and pepper on your own brisket, this pared-down rub is a great place to start. It'll give you a good flavor base without overpowering that brisket goodness.

3 tablespoons
  kosher salt

2 tablespoons freshly
  ground black pepper

1 tablespoon
  garlic powder

½ tablespoon
  minced onion

→ In a small mixing bowl, combine the salt, pepper, garlic powder, and minced onion. Mix all the spices together until well incorporated. Store any unused rub in the refrigerator in a resealable bag or airtight container for up to a week.

COOKING TIP: I designed this rub for brisket, but it'll work awesome for all your beef cooks. The simplicity complements meats while letting them show off their own flavor, so put this rub on a prime rib eye without worry.

Sweet and Spicy Rub

chicken, pork

PREP TIME: 5 minutes

MY PROFESSIONAL EXPERIENCE in the barbecue industry has been almost exclusively on the appliance end. By contrast, my experience in the spice and rub world is mostly as a home cook and amateur "taste consultant." One thing that I do know in the business of spices is this: You cannot beat a good sweet and spicy rub. Sweet and spicy rubs, used mostly for pork and poultry, are extremely popular. Sometimes a sweet-spicy combo is the only spice rub a given company will make. This recipe pulls the flavors of the best store-bought spices right into your own kitchen.

½ cup brown sugar

2 teaspoons kosher salt

2 teaspoons garlic powder

1 teaspoon onion powder

1 teaspoon smoked paprika

1 teaspoon freshly ground black pepper

½ teaspoon cayenne pepper

½ teaspoon oregano leaves

½ teaspoon ground ginger

½ teaspoon ground cumin

¼ teaspoon ground coriander

¼ teaspoon chili powder

→ In a small mixing bowl, combine the brown sugar, salt, garlic powder, onion powder, smoked paprika, black pepper, cayenne, oregano, ginger, cumin, coriander, and chili powder. Mix all the spices together well. Store any unused rub in a resealable bag or airtight container.

COOKING TIP: This spice is not too hot, so it is just fine for the kiddos. I am all too familiar with the cries of "It's too spicy!" from kids at the dinner table, so it's something I work to curb. Too much spice is good for Dad's palate, but bad for his home life—but if you like spicy, don't be afraid to up the amount of cayenne and chili powder.

Lemon-Pepper Seafood Rub

chicken, seafood

PREP TIME: 5 minutes

LEMON AND SEAFOOD go together like peanut butter and jelly—there just isn't a better combo out there. One of my favorite ways to kick that lemon flavor right into the seafood is with this lemon-pepper rub. Its zesty, lemon-garlic flavor works well with any seafood, from salmon to scallops to oysters and beyond.

2 tablespoons
   kosher salt

1 tablespoon
   granulated sugar

1 tablespoon
   lemon pepper

1 tablespoon
   garlic powder

1 teaspoon dillweed

→ In a small mixing bowl, combine the salt, sugar, lemon pepper, garlic powder, and dillweed. Mix all the spices together until well combined. Store any unused rub in a resealable bag or airtight container until ready to use.

COOKING TIP: I developed this rub for seafood, but also try using it on chicken—it's amazing for all kinds of cuts.

MEASUREMENT CONVERSIONS

VOLUME EQUIVALENTS	U.S. STANDARD	U.S. STANDARD (OUNCES)	METRIC (APPROXIMATE)
LIQUID	2 tablespoons	1 fl. oz.	30 mL
	¼ cup	2 fl. oz.	60 mL
	½ cup	4 fl. oz.	120 mL
	1 cup	8 fl. oz.	240 mL
	1½ cups	12 fl. oz.	355 mL
	2 cups or 1 pint	16 fl. oz.	475 mL
	4 cups or 1 quart	32 fl. oz.	1 L
	1 gallon	128 fl. oz.	4 L
DRY	⅛ teaspoon	–	0.5 mL
	¼ teaspoon	–	1 mL
	½ teaspoon	–	2 mL
	¾ teaspoon	–	4 mL
	1 teaspoon	–	5 mL
	1 tablespoon	–	15 mL
	¼ cup	–	59 mL
	⅓ cup	–	79 mL
	½ cup	–	118 mL
	⅔ cup	–	156 mL
	¾ cup	–	177 mL
	1 cup	–	235 mL
	2 cups or 1 pint	–	475 mL
	3 cups	–	700 mL
	4 cups or 1 quart	–	1 L
	½ gallon	–	2 L
	1 gallon	–	4 L

OVEN TEMPERATURES

FAHRENHEIT	CELSIUS (APPROXIMATE)
250°F	120°C
300°F	150°C
325°F	165°C
350°F	180°C
375°F	190°C
400°F	200°C
425°F	220°C
450°F	230°C

WEIGHT EQUIVALENTS

U.S. STANDARD	METRIC (APPROXIMATE)
½ ounce	15 g
1 ounce	30 g
2 ounces	60 g
4 ounces	115 g
8 ounces	225 g
12 ounces	340 g
16 ounces or 1 pound	455 g

RESOURCES

A-MAZE-N Products: *AMazeNProducts.com* The A-MAZE-N tube smokers are awesome to aid in smoke production on your pellet grill, as well as in place of a cold smoker.

Amazing Ribs: *AmazingRibs.com* Amazing Ribs is a longstanding barbecue website that has a seemingly endless amount of barbecue-related information and resources, including plenty on pellet grills.

Cheeky BBQ/Noah Cheek: *CheekyBBQ.com* Noah is extremely knowledgeable in the pellet-grill game, and he has an encyclopedic knowledge of meat and how it is prepared. He publishes his own recipes on this site.

FireBoard: *Fireboard.com* FireBoard Labs makes my favorite third-party thermometer. It uses WiFi and Bluetooth to send your grill and meat temperatures to the FireBoard app on your Android phone or iPhone.

Five Monkeys Barbecue Sauce: *FiveMonkeysBBQSauce.com* In my opinion, this is the best barbecue sauce on the market, and you can buy it here.

The Flavor Train/Chuck Matto: *TheFlavorTrain.com* Chuck is a barbecue genius, and he spends most of his time with pellet grills. I get tons of my barbecue ideas from his Instagram and TikTok (both @chucksflavortrain).

Franklin BBQ/Aaron Franklin: *FranklinBBQ.com* Aaron Franklin is the bona fide king of Texas barbecue. You won't find anything here specific to pellet grills, but he has tons of great info on barbecue and meat prep in general.

***Jay Ducote's Louisiana Outdoor Cooking* by Jay Ducote:** Jay Ducote is a Food Network star and, in my humble opinion, the king of Louisiana barbecue. Jay has made multiple appearances on ESPN's College GameDay, and he shares much of his tailgate knowledge in his book.

Master the Wood Pellet Grill: A Cookbook to Smoke Meats and More Like a Pro by Andrew Koster: My first pellet-grill cookbook was released in 2019. It's waiting for you when you're ready to take the next step in smoking meat, and it's a fantastic companion to this book, if I do say so myself.

Petromax: _Petromax.com_ Petromax is my choice for cast iron. It all comes preseasoned, and I can vouch for its high quality. Luckily for me (and for you), Petromax recently became available for purchase in the United States.

Pit Boss Grills: _PitBoss-Grills.com_ Pit Boss is the second-largest pellet-grill company and is growing quickly. Pit Boss has a diverse pellet grill and vertical smoker line. Visit its website for great pellet-grill education-related blog posts and videos.

Pit Boss Grill Owners Facebook group: _Facebook.com/groups/PitBoss_ This is similar to the Traeger group but specific to owners of Pit Boss grills. You must have a Facebook account to join this group.

Traeger Wood Pellet Grills: _TraegerGrills.com_ Traeger is the original manufacturer of the wood pellet grill. Its site features not only its line of grills but also a huge collection of pellet-grill recipes.

Traeger Grill Owners Facebook group: _Facebook.com/groups/TraegerGrill Owners_ Traeger Grill Owners is the largest pellet-grill forum on the internet. This forum is primarily targeted to Traeger owners specifically, but other grill owners are welcome participants. You do have to have a Facebook account to join this group.

Weber Grills: _Weber.com_ Weber, the world's largest grill distributor, jumped on the pellet-grill bandwagon in 2020. Though new to pellet grills, Weber has a vast array of barbecue resources for grillers of all skill levels.

INDEX

ACKNOWLEDGMENTS

My love and knowledge of barbeque comes from having the opportunity to be absorbed in it as part of my everyday work. I'd like to thank Dan, Jeff, and Jordan Thiessen, who give me and my dad, George, the ability to do what we love and enjoy every day. Had I not come to work at Dansons, where I reignited my passion for smoking, this book wouldn't have been possible.

My dad has had the greatest impact on my career in barbeque, but I also owe my thanks to Joe Traeger, Bobby Martin, and Mark Kosiba. Each of these men has helped me grow in the pellet-grill industry and stoked my passion for helping others learn to grill.

Family is more important to me than anything, and most of all my family made this book possible. Pepe, Luke, Blake, Julie, Mom, and Dad—thank you for all you have done for me in the past year. It was a rough one, and you pulled me through it. Bri, Chloe, and Chanelle, I love you and always appreciate support—and all the help with amateur photography.

ABOUT THE AUTHOR

ANDREW KOSTER is a pellet-grill aficionado who has spent most of his life smelling of wood-fired smoke. He is the author of *Master the Wood Pellet Grill: A Cookbook to Smoke Meats and More Like a Pro*, as well as the former customer service manager of Traeger, Pit Boss, and Louisiana Grills. On top of helping countless customers learn and conquer the pellet grill, Andrew has also assisted in the development of multiple pellet grills, including the Traeger Timberline, Pit Boss Platinum Series, and Louisiana Grills Black Label and Founders Series.

Andrew currently works as a member of the product team at Dansons, maker of Pit Boss and Louisiana Grills, and lives in Silverton, Oregon, with his wife, Chanelle, and his three children, Brianna, Chloe, and Andrew Jr.

CPSIA information can be obtained
at www.ICGtesting.com
Printed in the USA
JSHW010035310821
18288JS00007B/9